John R. Sweney, Henry Lake Gilmour, William J. Kirkpatrick

Winning Songs

For Use in Meetings for Christian Worship or Work

John R. Sweney, Henry Lake Gilmour, William J. Kirkpatrick

Winning Songs

For Use in Meetings for Christian Worship or Work

ISBN/EAN: 9783337290139

Printed in Europe, USA, Canada, Australia, Japan

Cover: Foto ©Thomas Meinert / pixelio.de

More available books at **www.hansebooks.com**

WINNING SONGS:

FOR USE IN

MEETINGS FOR CHRISTIAN WORSHIP OR WORK.

EDITORS:

JNO. R. SWENEY, WM. J. KIRKPATRICK, AND H. L. GILMOUR.

He that winneth souls is wise."
—Pr. 11: 30.

PHILADELPHIA:

Published by JOHN J. HOOD, 1024 Arch St.

Copyright, 1892, by John J. Hood.

I

THERE is a song which a child can sing,
    A song which is sure to win;
Simple and sweet, its refrain will bring
    A sigh from the heart of sin.

II

It tells of Christ, and the Father's love,
    It tells of the heavenly rest;—
Of the smile of God, and the home above,
    And the good forever blest.

III

These tender songs, sung with love aglow,
    And soft with the spirit's sigh;—
Awaken thoughts of the long ago,
    And the loved ones in the sky.

IV

So may these songs, in their winnings, win
    Great hosts from every clime;
And winning all from the paths of sin,
    Bring the victor's song sublime.

                                            E. H. STOKES.
Ocean Grove, N. J., May, 1892.

COPYRIGHT NOTICE.

To PRINT, for sale or otherwise, any copyright hymn of this collection, unless written permission shall have been obtained, is an infringement of copyright.
                                              THE PUBLISHER.

WINNING SONGS.

Fed Upon the Finest of the Wheat.

F. A. G. Ps. lxxxi: 16. F. A. GRAVES.

1. Hun- gry, Lord, for thy word of truth, Sitting at my Saviour's feet;
2. Work for the Mas- ter I will do, Trusting in his strength so great;
3. Then to the har - vest let us go, Bugles sounding no retreat;

Ris - ing, gleaning, just like Ruth, Feed me on the finest of the wheat.
Liv - ing in his pastures new, Feed me on the finest of the wheat.
Workers for Je - sus, he wants you Fed up- on the finest of the wheat.

CHORUS.

Bread of life it is now to me, Hon - ey, milk and meat;

In thy love I will ev - er be Fed upon the finest of the wheat.

Copyright, 1892, by John J. Hood.

(3)

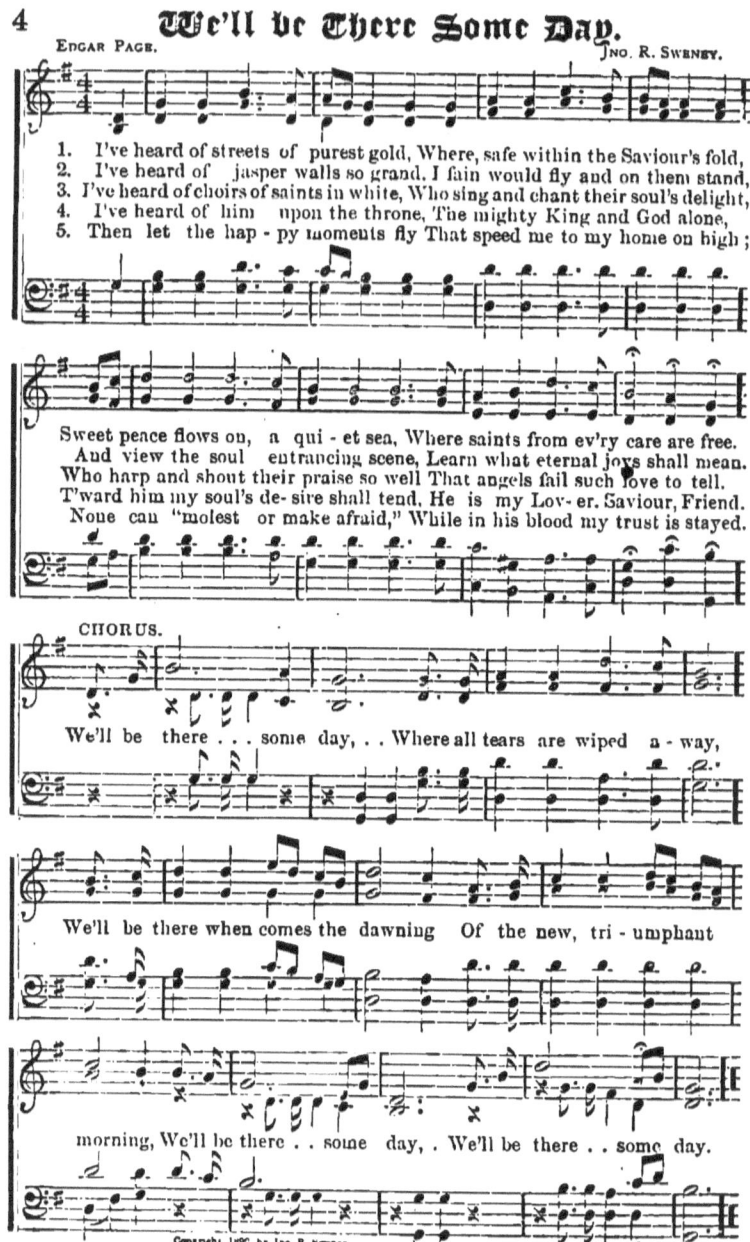

O for a Heart Whiter than Snow. 5

E. E. Hewitt.   Wm. J. Kirkpatrick.

1. O for a heart that is whiter than snow! Kept, ever kept, 'neath the
2. O for a heart that is whiter than snow! Calm in the peace that he
3. O for a heart that is whiter than snow! With the pure flame of the
4. O for a heart that is whiter than snow! Then in his grace and his

life-giv-ing flow; Cleansed from all pas-sion, self-seeking, and pride,
loves to be-stow; Dai-ly refreshed by the heav-en-ly dews,
Spir-it a-glow; Filled with the love that is true and sin-cere,
knowledge to grow; Grow-ing like him who my pat-tern shall be,

CHORUS.

Washed in the fountain of Cal-va-ry's tide. O for a heart
Read-y for ser-vice whene'er he shall choose.
Love that is a-ble to ban-ish all fear.
Till in his beau-ty my King I shall see.

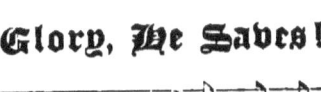

Glory, He Saves!

F. A. B.   F. A. BLACKMER.

1. Glo - ry to Je - sus, he saves e - ven me! All my guilt
2. Wand'ring he found me a - far from the fold, Per - ish - ing
3. Safe - ly and sweet - ly he keeps me each day, Gent - ly, so
4. Bless - ed com - pan - ion- ship! cheer- ing 'me so! Sweet - er and

nail - ing to Cal - va - ry's tree; Paid is the debt and my
there in the dark - ness and cold; Half of his good - ness can
gent - ly he leads all the way; An- swers of peace sends he
sweet - er each day shall it grow, Till to be like him I

soul is set free, Glo - ry to Je - sus, he saves!
nev - er be told, Glo - ry to Je - sus, he saves!
down when I pray, Glo - ry to Je - sus, he saves!
joy - ful - ly go, Glo - ry to Je - sus, he saves!

CHORUS.

Glo- ry, he saves! wondrously saves! Saves a poor sinner like me;

Glo - ry, he saves! wondrously saves! Glory to Je - sus, he saves!

Copyright, 189 , by John J. Hood

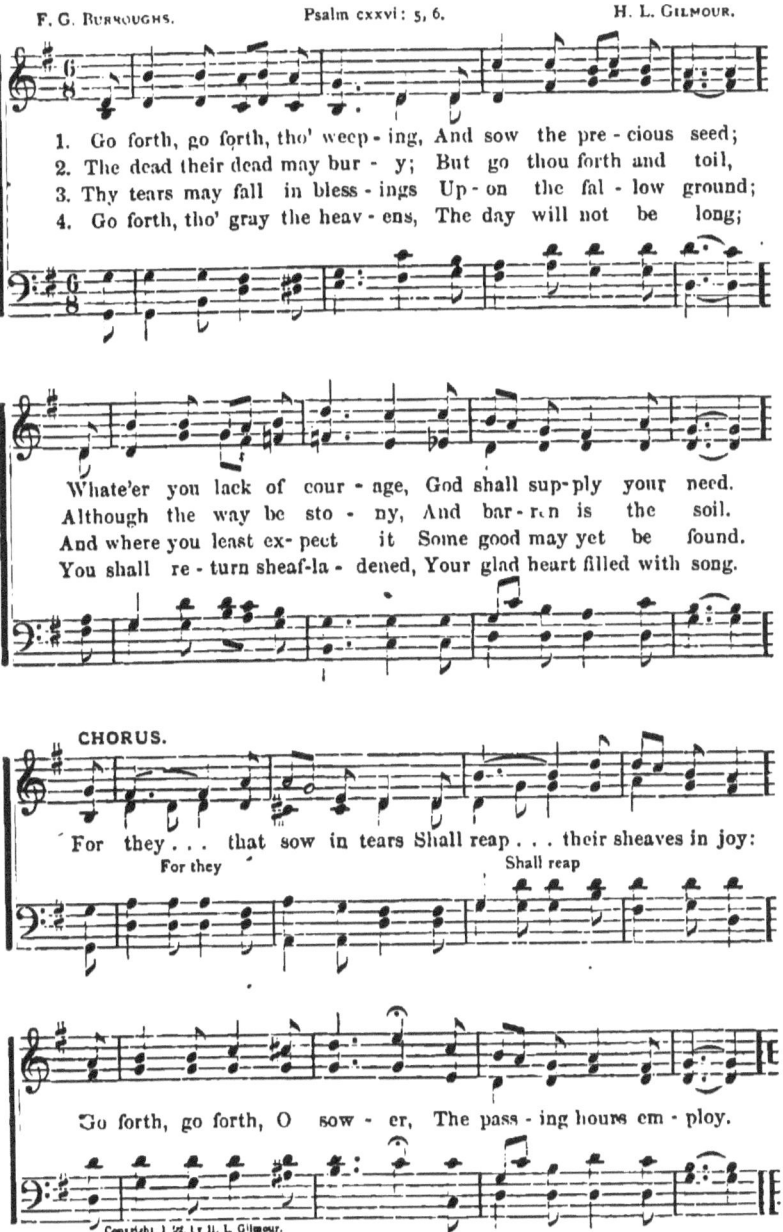

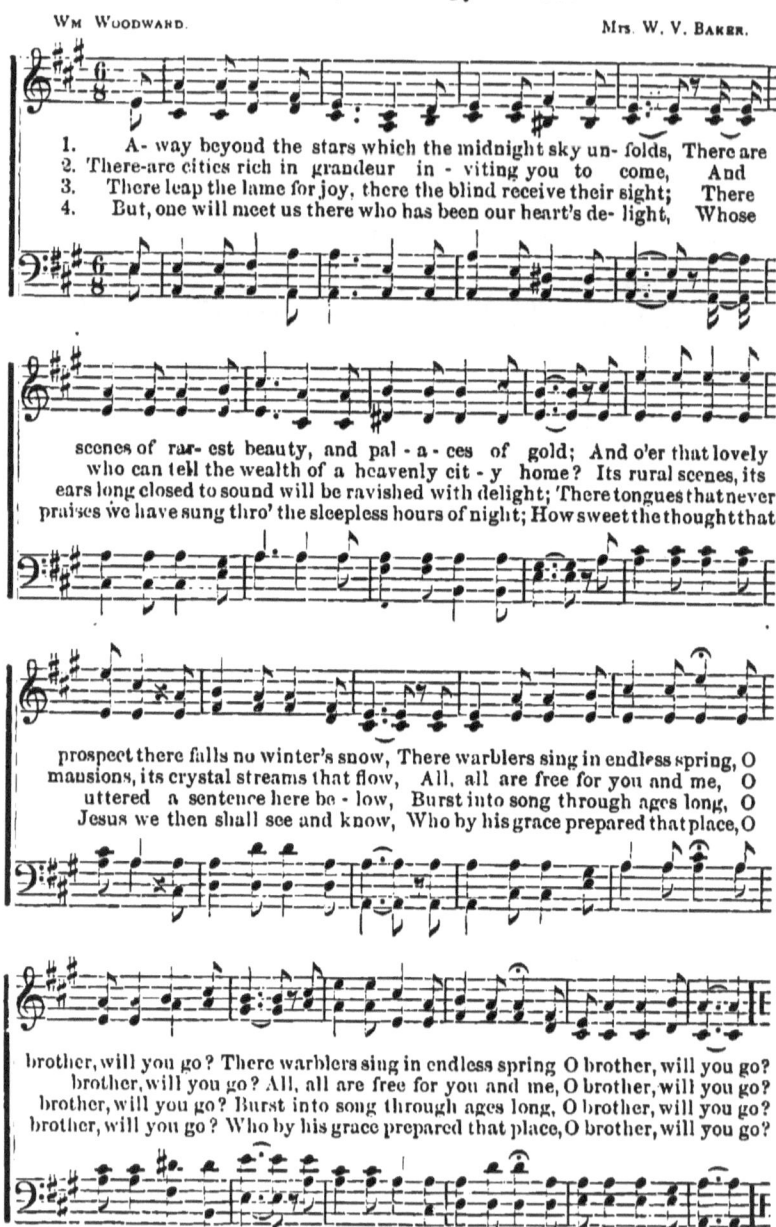

14. We'll Build on the Rock.

Mrs. E. W. Chapman. J. H. Tenney.

1. 'Tis the purpose of love di-vine That each life be of heavenly build,
2. On the Rock we will build in faith, And our hope shall in him a-bide,
3. 'Tis a Rock that can never fail, No rude tempest our house can harm,

In the kingdom of light to shine, When free grace shall the structure gild.
For we know that the scripture saith, "As by fire shall our work be tried."
Though the storms and the winds assail, Not a shock can our hearts a-larm.

CHORUS.

So we'll build on the Rock Christ Jesus, 'Tis a firm foundation stone,
yes, we'll build,
Yes, we'll build on the mighty Rock of Ages, We'll build on him a-lone.
We'll

Copyright, 1006, by John J Hood

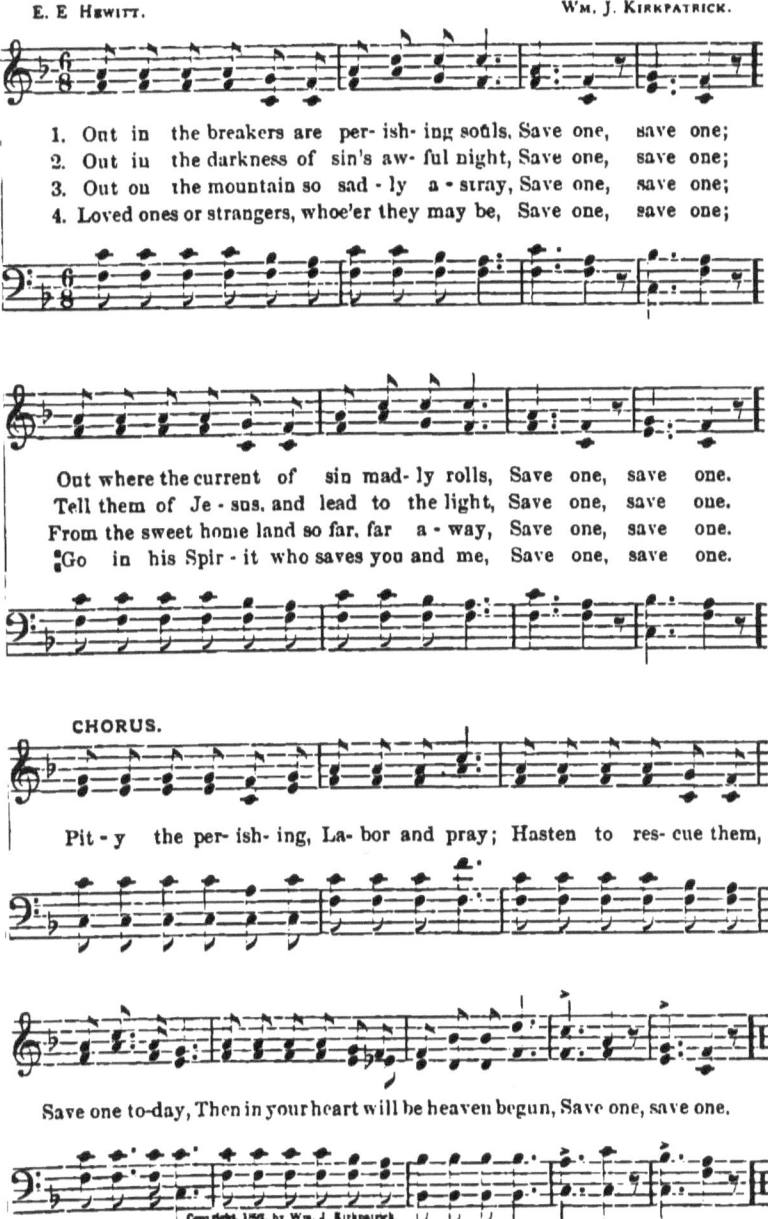

All Bright Above.

Mrs. Mary D. James. Wm. J. Kirkpatrick.

1. I see the bright, ef- fulgent rays Out beaming from the Saviour's face;
2. Oh, blessed vision! glad surprise! It breaks upon my wond'ring eyes,—
3. Triumphant Christ! all conqu'ring King! Thy praises I delight to sing;

No dark'ning clouds obscure the sight Of his sweet smile—my Life, my Light.
The Sun of Righteousness divine, In whom the Father's glories shine.
Thy glo-ry shines around me here, My path is bright, my sky is clear.

REFRAIN. *Not too fast.*

I am mounting on wings, I am soaring on high, Where the sun's ever shining in unclouded sky, In the joy of his presence, the smiles of his love; Oh, glo-ry to Je-sus! 'tis all bright above; 'Tis all bright above, 'tis

Copyright, 1884, by Wm. J. Kirkpatrick.

All Bright Above.—CONCLUDED.

all bright a-bove, Oh, glo-ry to Je-sus! 'tis all bright a-bove.

What Must I Do to be Saved?

"Believe on the Lord Jesus Christ, and thou shalt be saved."
Acts xvi. 31.

E. E. Hewitt. L. L. Pickett.

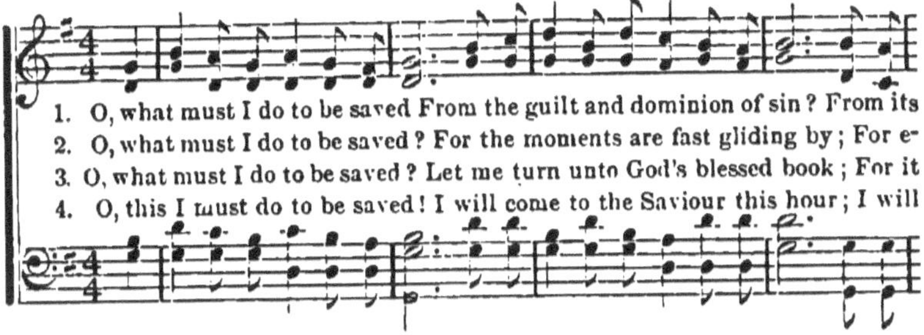

1. O, what must I do to be saved From the guilt and dominion of sin? From its
2. O, what must I do to be saved? For the moments are fast gliding by; For e-
3. O, what must I do to be saved? Let me turn unto God's blessed book; For it
4. O, this I must do to be saved! I will come to the Saviour this hour; I will

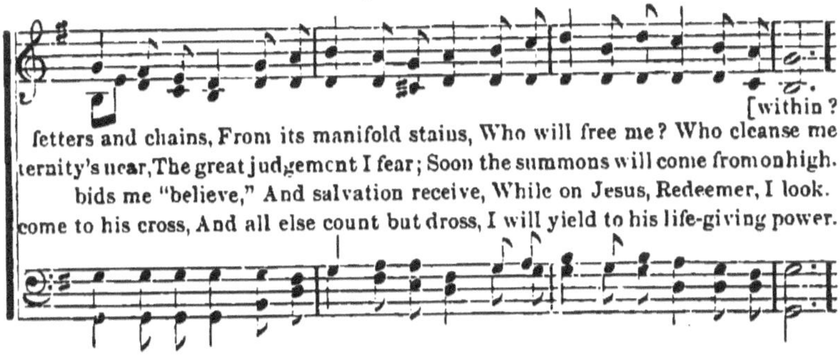

[within?

fetters and chains, From its manifold stains, Who will free me? Who cleanse me
ternity's near, The great judgement I fear; Soon the summons will come from on high.
bids me "believe," And salvation receive, While on Jesus, Redeemer, I look.
come to his cross, And all else count but dross, I will yield to his life-giving power.

CHORUS.

O, what must I do? O, what must I do? O, what must I do to be saved?

Copyright, 1891, by Wm. J. Kirkpatrick. Winning Songs—B

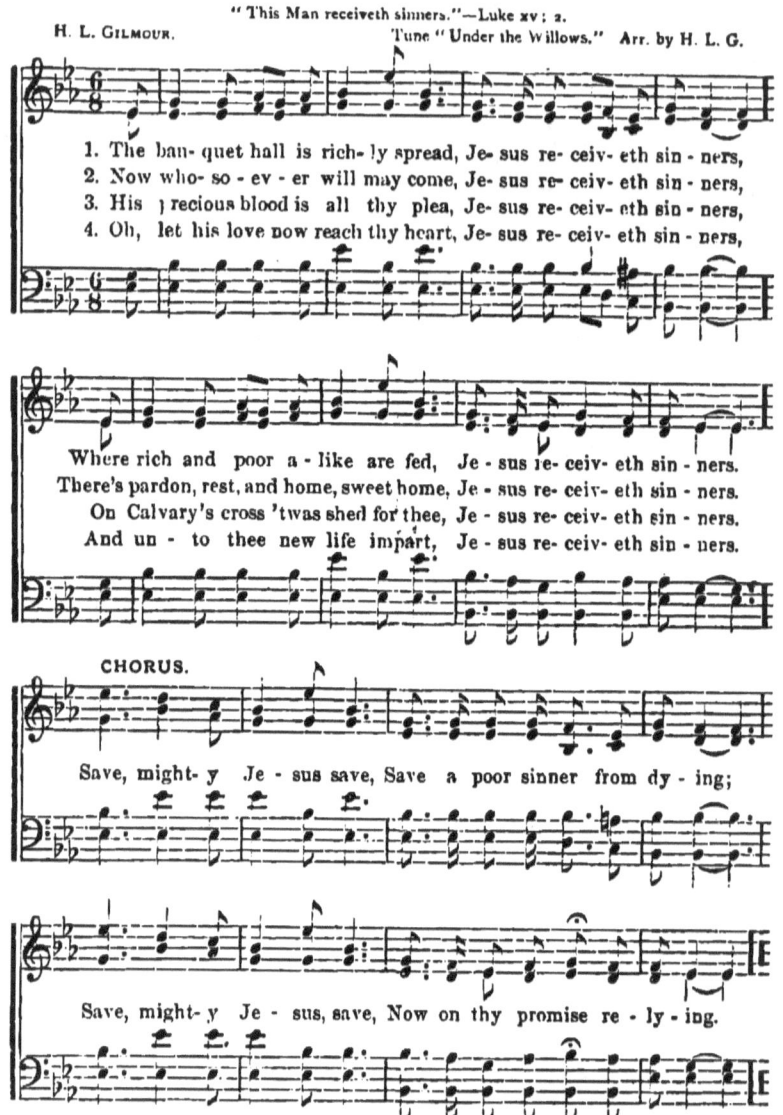

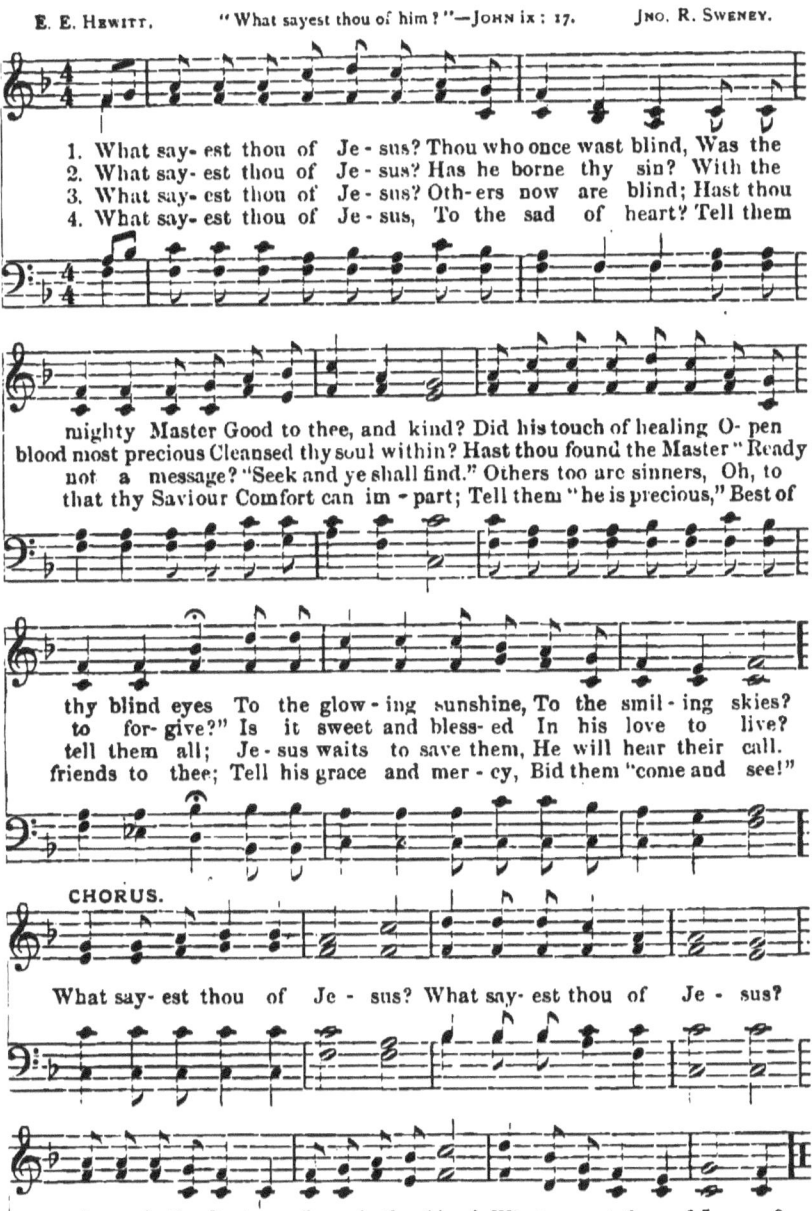

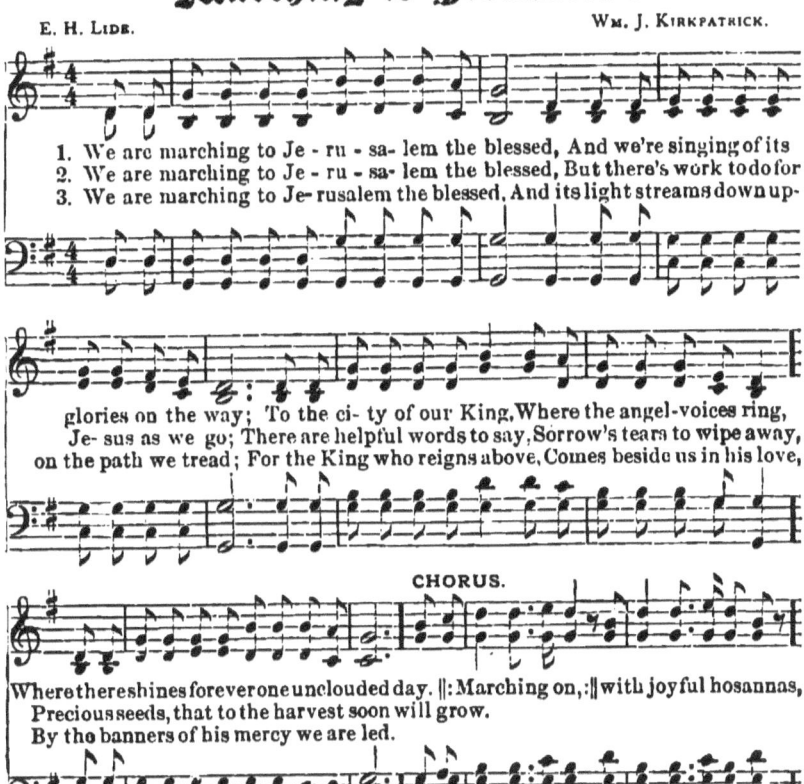

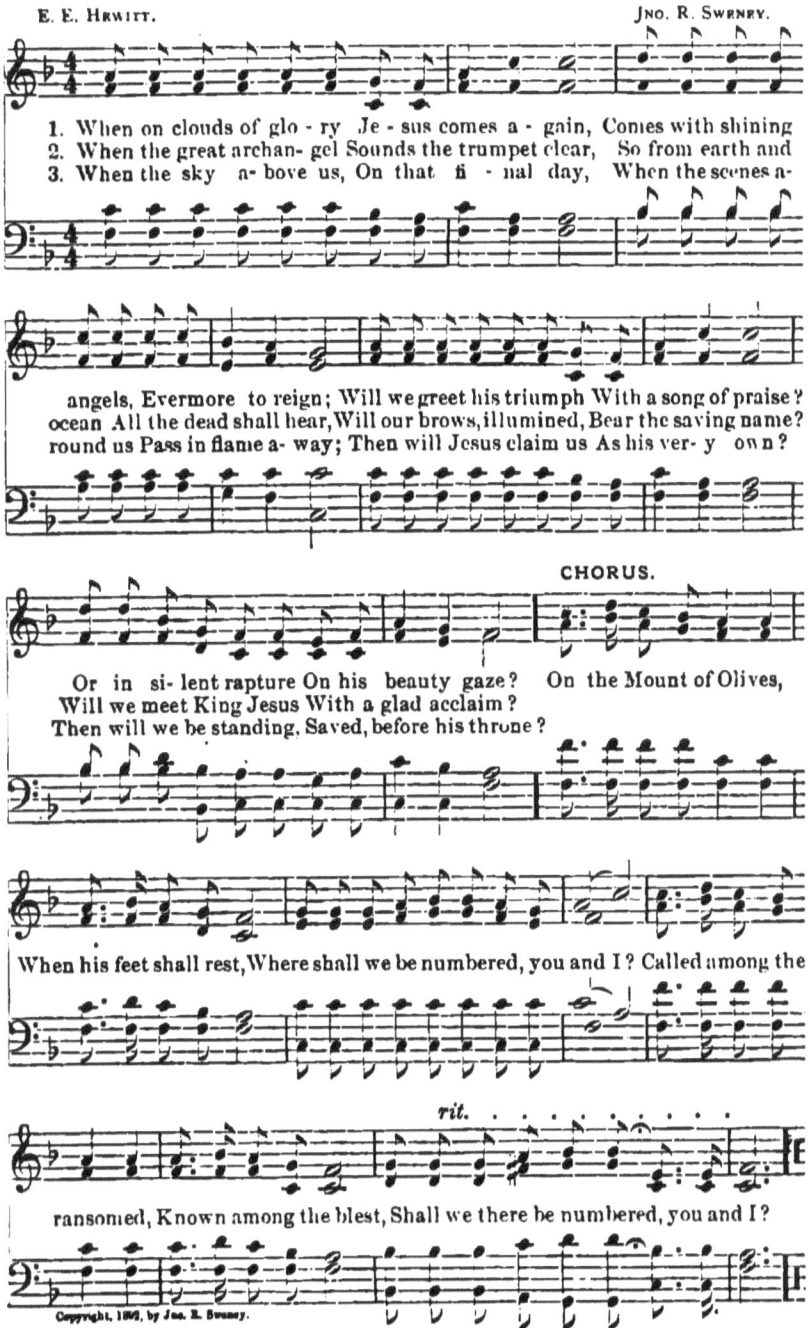

28. He'll Mention Them no More.

"They shall not be mentioned unto him."—Ezek. xvii: 22.

E. E. Hewitt.
Jno. R. Sweney.

1. My soul sings glory all the way, For Jesus took my sins away;
2. Oh, wondrous grace, so rich and free, That mentions not my sins to me,
3. But since he shows such grace to me, Let not his love forgotten be;
4. My soul sings glory all the way To yonder land of cloudless day,

With precious blood they're covered o'er, He'll mention them no more.
Since Jesus in redeeming love, Brought mercy from above.
Oh, let my life its tribute bring, My heart exultant sing.
And when I reach that happy shore, I'll praise him evermore.

CHORUS.

My sins . . . . . are all taken away, ...
My sins are all taken away,
My sins are all taken away,

My sins . . . . . are all taken away; . . . . .
My sins are all taken away,
My sins are all taken away;

Oh, glory to his name! Oh, glory to his name! My

Copyright, 1892, by Jno. R. Sweney.

We'll Mention Them, etc.—CONCLUDED.

sins are all tak-en a-way, tak-en a-way. . . . . . tak-en a-way.

Happy in the Lord My Saviour.

HENRIETTA E. BLAIR. WM. J. KIRKPATRICK.

1. Happy in the Lord my Sa-viour, Happy as a heart can be;
2. Happy in the Lord my Sa-viour, Trusting him from hour to hour;
3. Happy in the Lord my Sa-viour, Happy when the skies are bright;
4. Glo-ry to the Lord my Sa-viour, Glo-ry to the Lord my King;

Fine.

Walking in the light that shin-eth Ev-er like a star for me.
Leaning on his arm of mer-cy, Fearing not the tempter's power.
Happy though the clouds may gather, Happy in the deepest night.
Happy in a full sal-va-tion, Glo-ry to his name I sing.

D.S.—"Blessed are the poor in spir-it," "Blessed are the pure in heart."

CHORUS. *D.S.*

Precious are the words of com-fort, Whispered from the world apart;

Copyright, 1892, by Wm. J. Kirkpatrick.

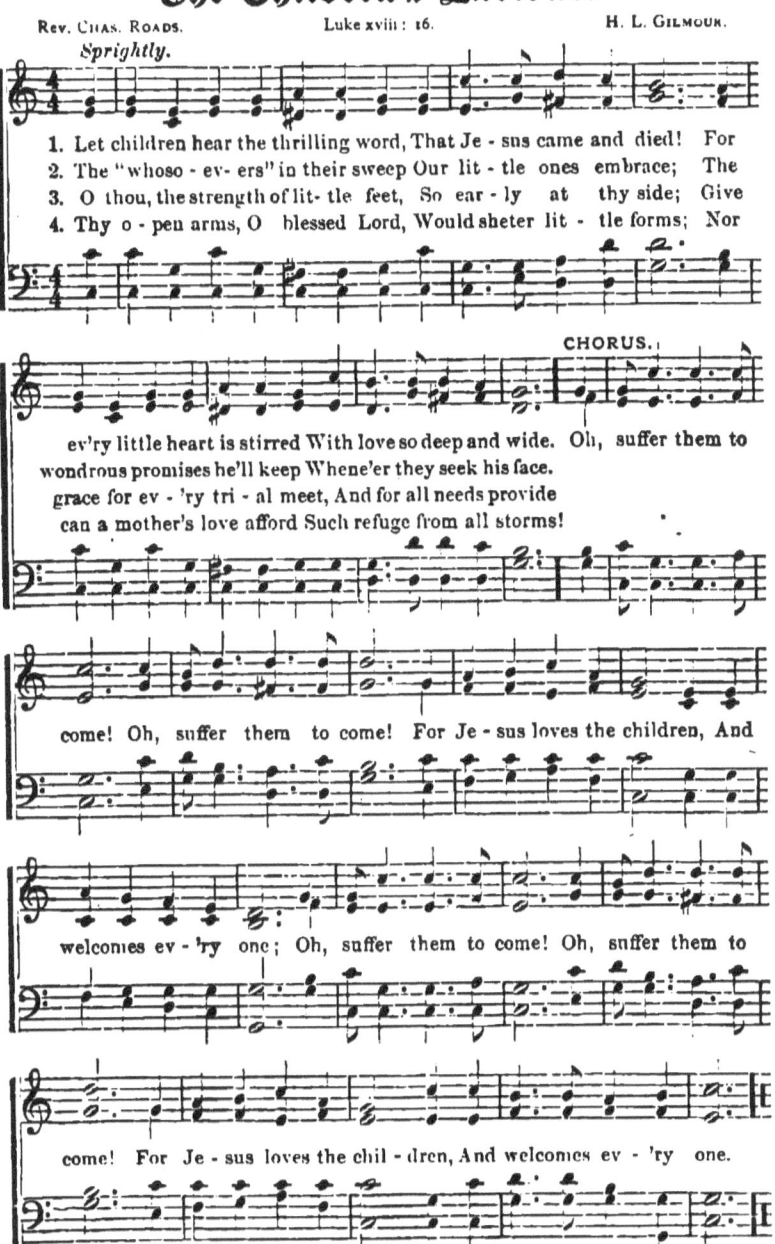

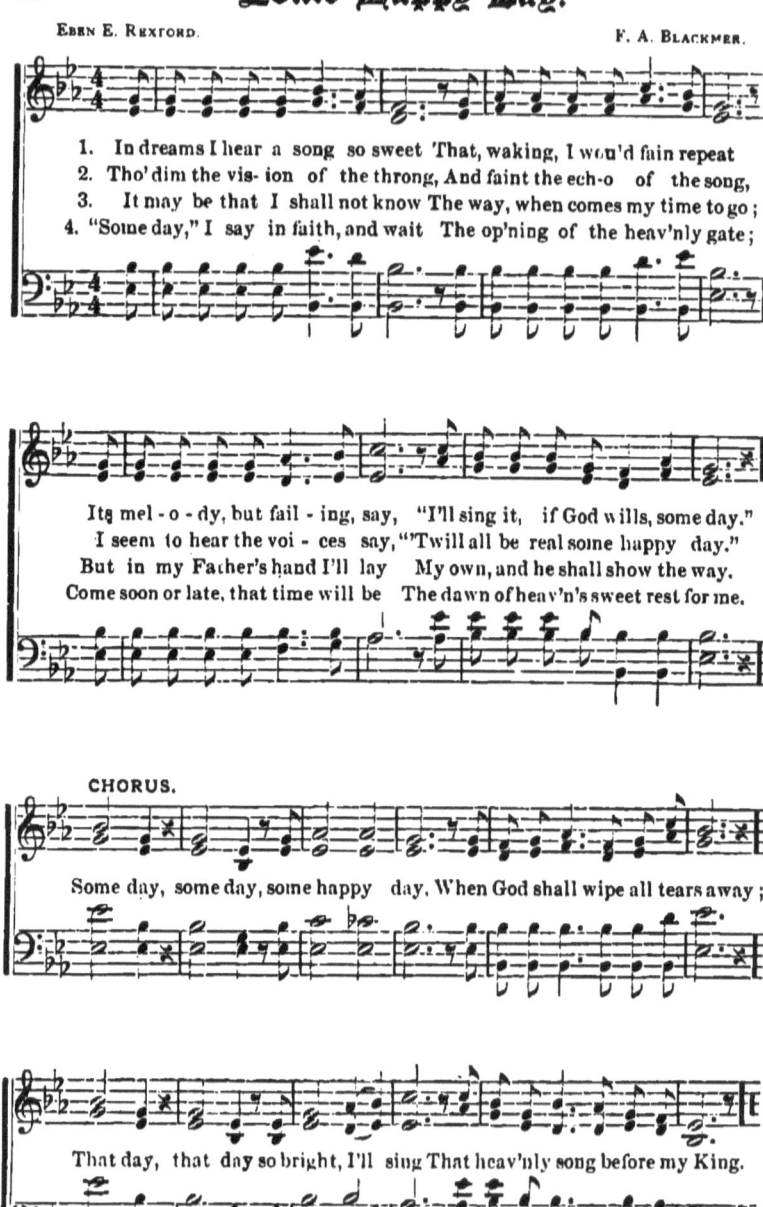

Saviour, I'm Trusting.—CONCLUDED.

poco ritard.

Led to the glo-ri-ous fountain, Saviour, I'm trusting in thee.

Take this Heart of Mine.

E. E. Hewitt.   Jno. R. Sweney.

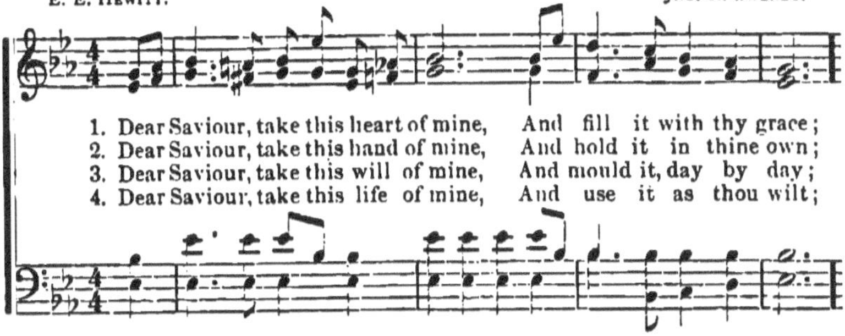

1. Dear Saviour, take this heart of mine, And fill it with thy grace;
2. Dear Saviour, take this hand of mine, And hold it in thine own;
3. Dear Saviour, take this will of mine, And mould it, day by day;
4. Dear Saviour, take this life of mine, And use it as thou wilt;

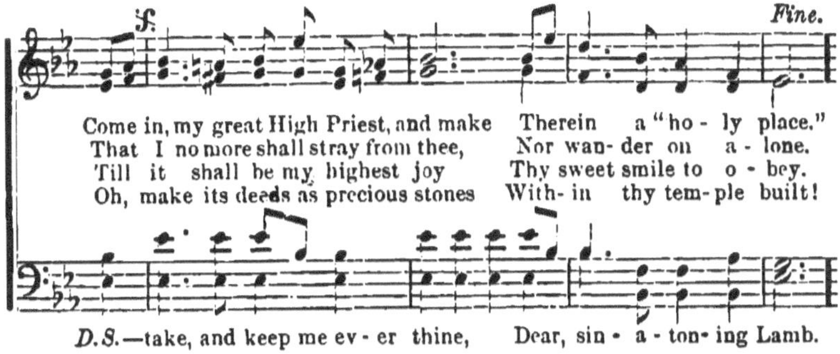

Come in, my great High Priest, and make Therein a "ho-ly place."
That I no more shall stray from thee, Nor wan-der on a-lone.
Till it shall be my highest joy Thy sweet smile to o-bey.
Oh, make its deeds as precious stones With-in thy tem-ple built!

D.S.—take, and keep me ev-er thine, Dear, sin-a-ton-ing Lamb.

CHORUS.   *D.S.*

To thee, my Saviour, I resign All that I have and am; O

Copyright, 1882, by John R. Sweney.

40. Sweet Rest There.

"There remaineth therefore a rest to the people of God."—Heb. iv: 9.

F. A. B.
F. A. BLACKMER.

1. How precious the tho't, when with sorrows we meet, There'll be sweet rest there!
2. Tho' bowed 'neath the burdens that here so oppress, There'll be sweet rest there;
3. Look up, soul bereft, and remem-ber ere long There'll be sweet rest there;
4. On that quiet shore, past the mad breakers' foam, There'll be sweet rest there;
5. Earth's weariness soon shall forev - er be past, There'll be sweet rest there.

Tho' oft faints the spir-it, and fal - ter the feet, There'll be sweet rest there;
Our Saviour on earth felt the same weariness, There'll be sweet rest there;
The sigh of the mourner shall merge into song, There'll be sweet rest there;
No sorrow of earth shall be felt in that home, There'll be sweet rest there.
The rest that "remaineth" we'll enter at last, There'll be sweet rest there.

m CHORUS. *p*

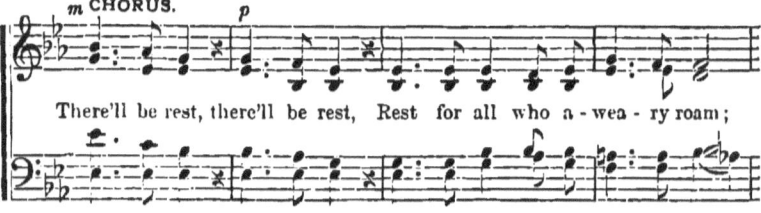

There'll be rest, there'll be rest, Rest for all who a - wea - ry roam;

m *p*

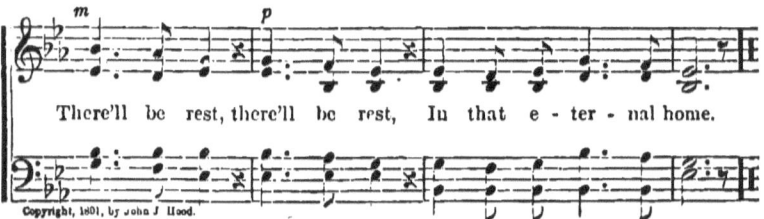

There'll be rest, there'll be rest, In that e - ter - nal home.

Copyright, 1891, by John J. Hood.

42. A Talk about Jesus.

E. E. Hewitt.   Jno. R. Sweney.

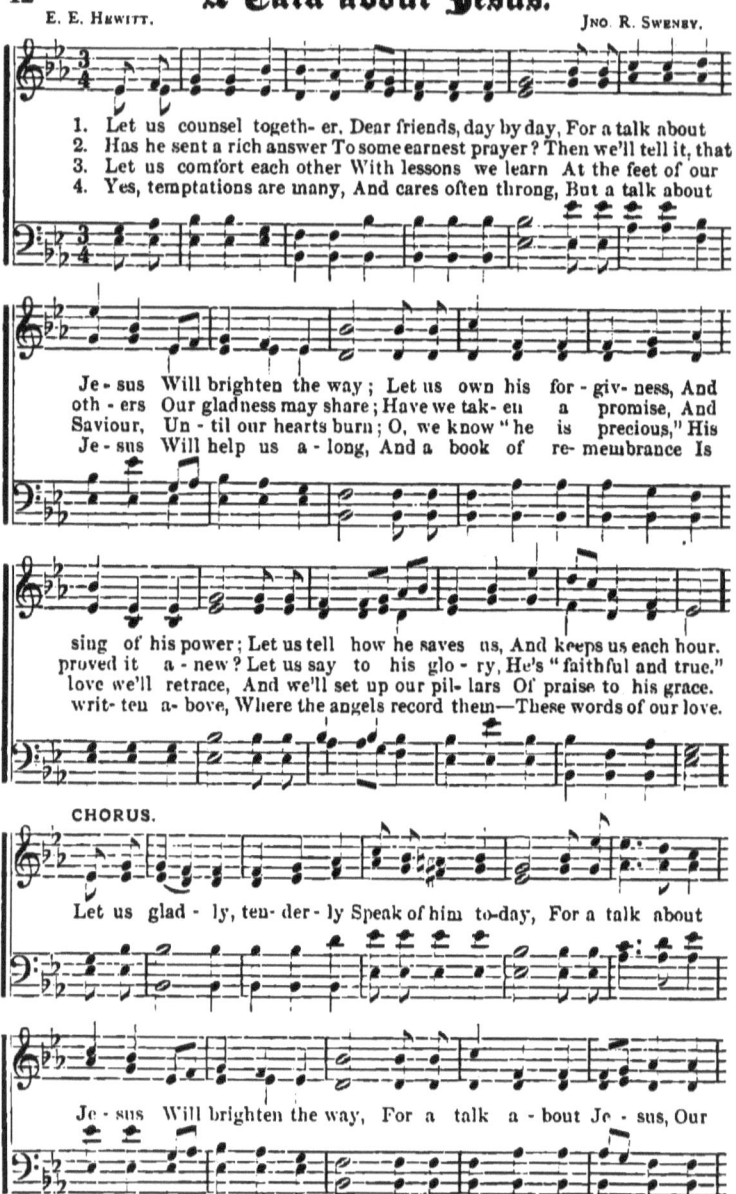

1. Let us counsel togeth- er, Dear friends, day by day, For a talk about
2. Has he sent a rich answer To some earnest prayer? Then we'll tell it, that
3. Let us comfort each other With lessons we learn At the feet of our
4. Yes, temptations are many, And cares often throng, But a talk about

Je- sus Will brighten the way; Let us own his for - giv- ness, And
oth - ers Our gladness may share; Have we tak- en a promise, And
Saviour, Un - til our hearts burn; O, we know "he is precious," His
Je - sus Will help us a - long, And a book of re- membrance Is

sing of his power; Let us tell how he saves us, And keeps us each hour.
proved it a - new? Let us say to his glo - ry, He's "faithful and true."
love we'll retrace, And we'll set up our pil- lars Of praise to his grace.
writ- ten a- bove, Where the angels record them—These words of our love.

CHORUS.

Let us glad - ly, ten- der - ly Speak of him to-day, For a talk about
Je - sus Will brighten the way, For a talk a - bout Je - sus, Our

Copyright, 1876, by Jno R. Sweney.

A Talk about Jesus.—CONCLUDED.

dear, loving Saviour, A sweet talk about Jesus Will brighten the way.

Nearer to Thy Side.

IDA L. REED.   WM. J. KIRKPATRICK.

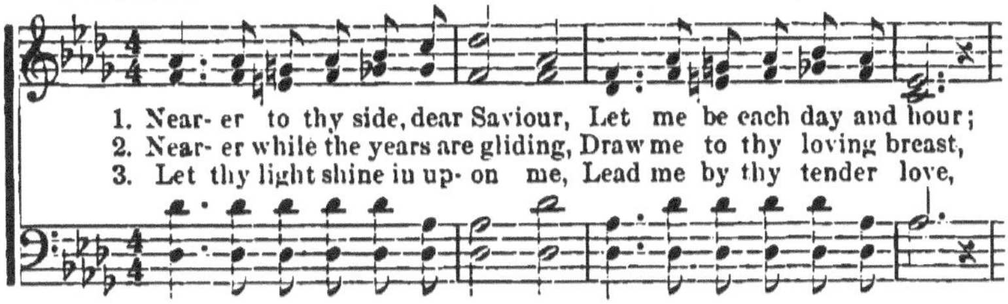

1. Near-er to thy side, dear Saviour, Let me be each day and hour;
2. Near-er while the years are gliding, Draw me to thy loving breast,
3. Let thy light shine in up-on me, Lead me by thy tender love,

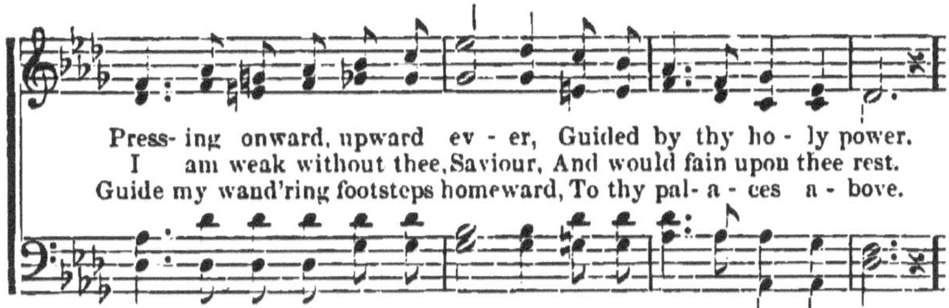

Press-ing onward, upward ev-er, Guided by thy ho-ly power.
I am weak without thee, Saviour, And would fain upon thee rest.
Guide my wand'ring footsteps homeward, To thy pal-a-ces a-bove.

CHORUS.

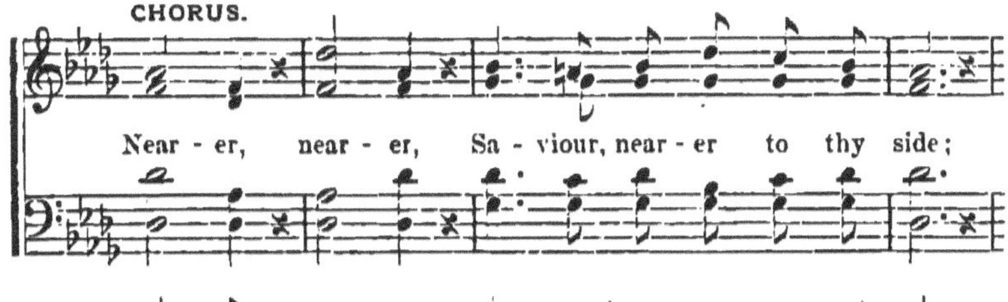

Near-er, near-er, Sa-viour, near-er to thy side;

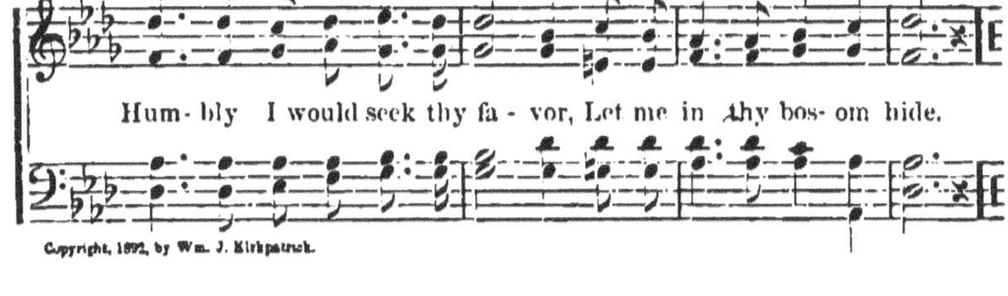

Hum-bly I would seek thy fa-vor, Let me in thy bos-om hide.

Copyright, 1892, by Wm. J. Kirkpatrick.

44. Have Courage to Say Yes.

W. S. Martin.   J. H. Tenney.

1. While Jesus is calling, oh, do not delay; He's longing to bless you, receive him to-day; Wait not till to-morrow, *now* trust in his love, Say, yes loud and strong;
2. Say yes in the darkness, say yes in the light, Say yes when the sun is obscured from thy sight; Look up, for above thee the sun soon will shine, The clouds are dispersing, the vic-t'ry is thine.
3. Say yes in thy weakness, for Christ is thy strength, Tho' foes may oppress thee he'll help thee at length; Fight on, then, my brother, till vic-t'ry is won, And thou in his presence shall hear the "well done."

CHORUS.

Yes, blessed Master, thy promise I'll prove. Say yes to thy Saviour, say yes loud and strong; Have courage, my brother, to stand 'gainst the wrong; Say yes, and then walk in the strength of the Lord, Say yes, and then live by the power of his word.

Copyright, 1889, by John J Hood.

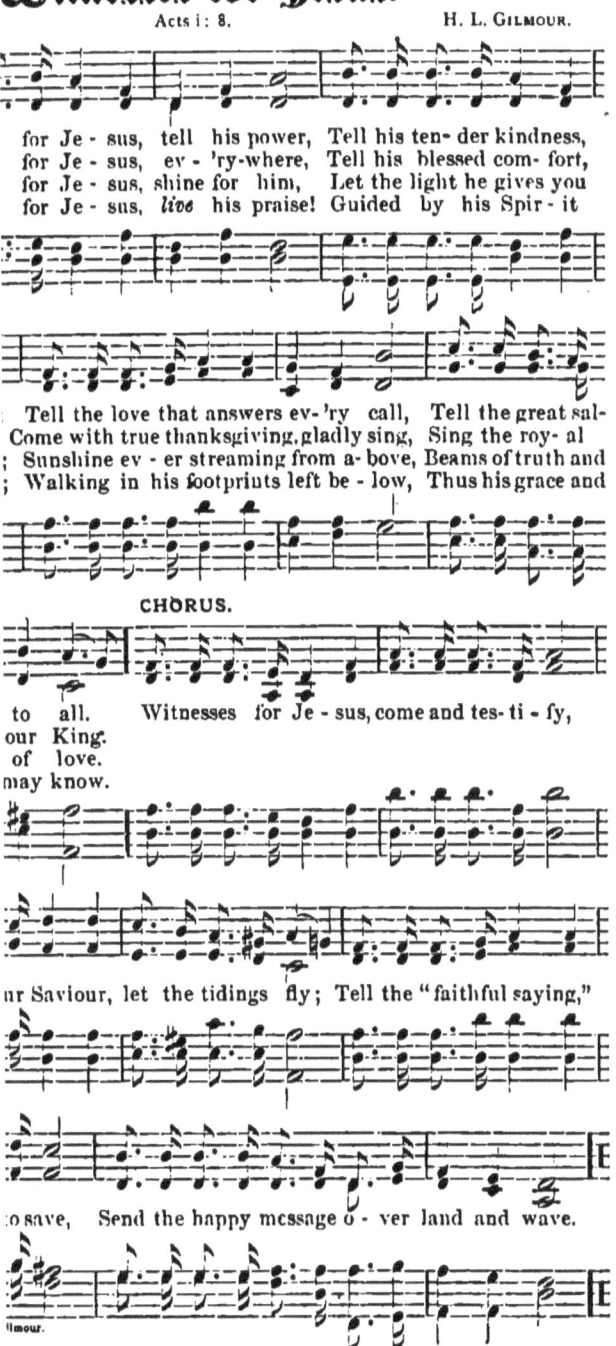

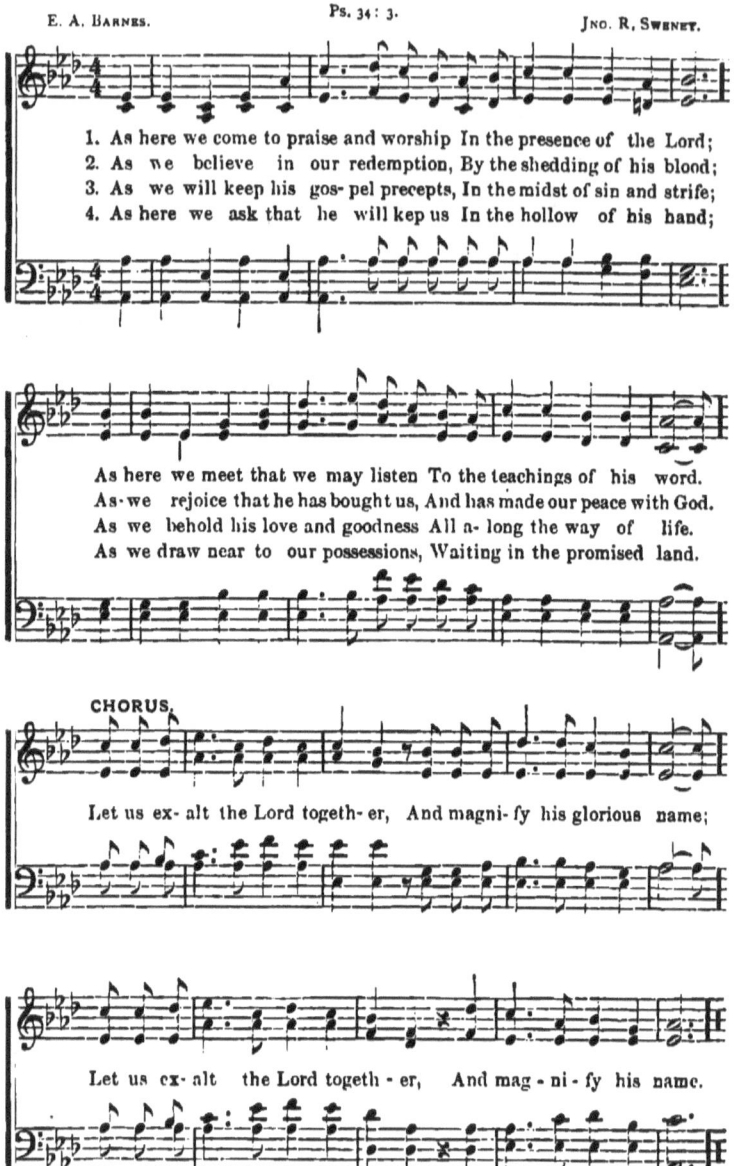

Marching with Gladness.—CONCLUDED. 51

banner, how calm and blest He mak - eth his own to rest.
how   calm and blest   He maketh his own to rest.

Rest, Weary Heart.

L. H. EDMUNDS.   JNO. R. SWENEY.

1. Rest, weary heart, For Je- sus bids thee rest; Sweet comfort find Up-
2. Come, with thy fears, With all thy griefs to-day; His gen-tle hand Will
3. Tell him thy need, Yea, o - pen all thy heart; His mighty love Will
4. Rest, weary heart, Upon thy heavenly Friend; Till morning break, And

CHORUS.

on his loving breast.   Rest, rest, weary heart, rest, Rest, rest, weary heart, rest,
wipe thy tears away.
healing balm impart.
earthly sorrows end.

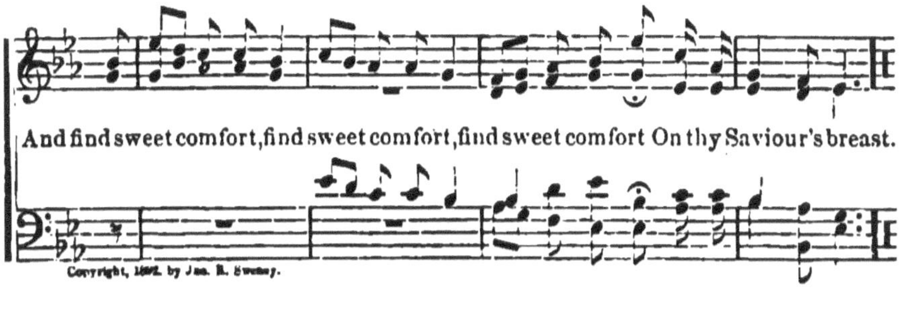

And find sweet comfort, find sweet comfort, find sweet comfort On thy Saviour's breast.

Copyright, 1892, by Jno. R. Sweney.

52. Never Will the Lord Forsake Us.

"He hath said, I will never leave thee, nor forsake thee."

E. E. Hewitt.   Heb. xiii. 5.   Jno. R. Sweney.

1. Never will the Lord forsake us, Blessed words, that echo down the years!
2. Never will the Lord forsake us, Earthly friends may leave and joys decay,
3. Never will the Lord forsake us, Tho' afar the wand'ring feet have stray'd,
4. Never will the Lord forsake us, There's a light upon the silent tide,

And there's not a cloud sweeps o'er our sky, But this bow of hope appears.
But the friend who gave his life to save, Will go with us all the way.
He will seek, will guide, the souls he loves, He will keep; "be not a-fraid."
For we know his "ev-er-lasting arms," Bear us on to Canaan's side.

CHORUS.

Blessed words God hath said! In his book, in his book we have read,

Never will he forsake, While his promise we take; Let the heart's hallelujahs awake.

Copyright, 1891, by Jno. R. Sweney.

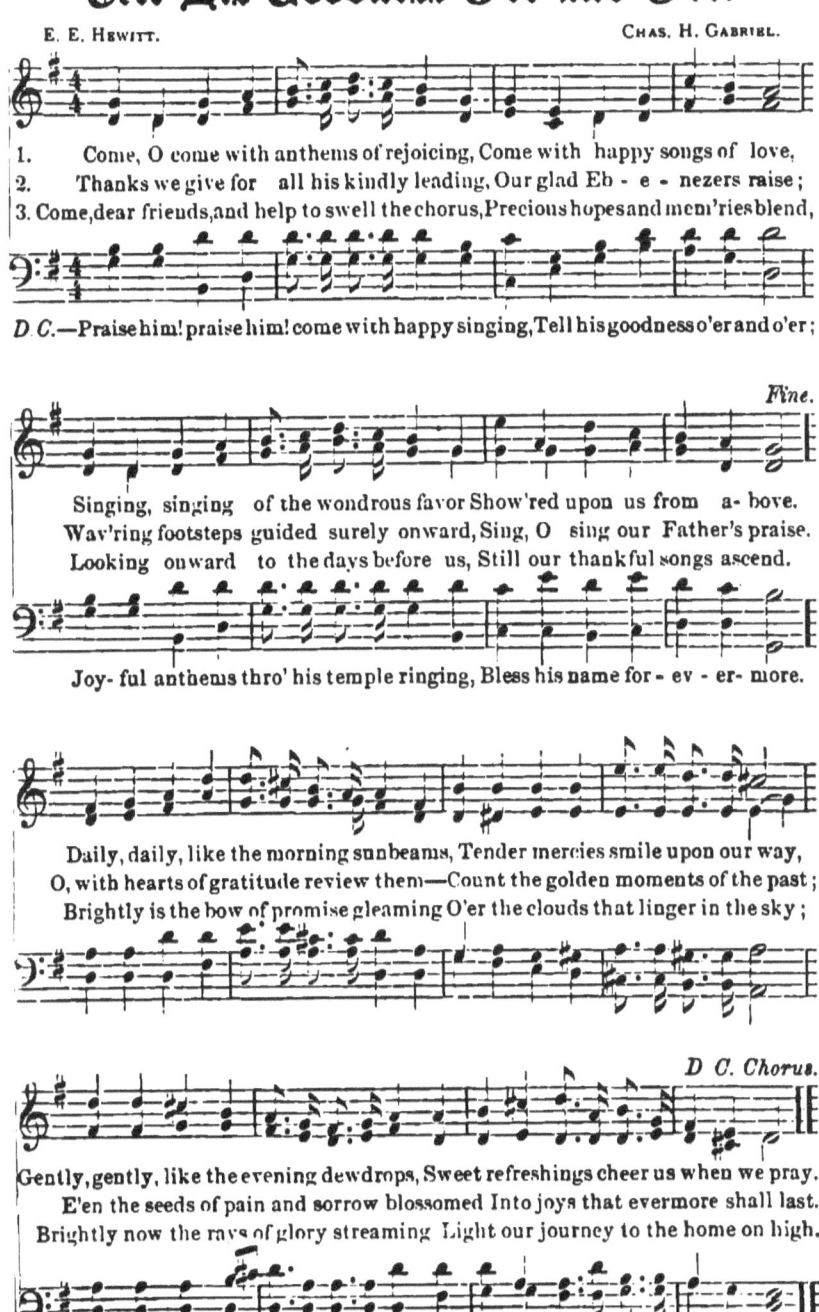

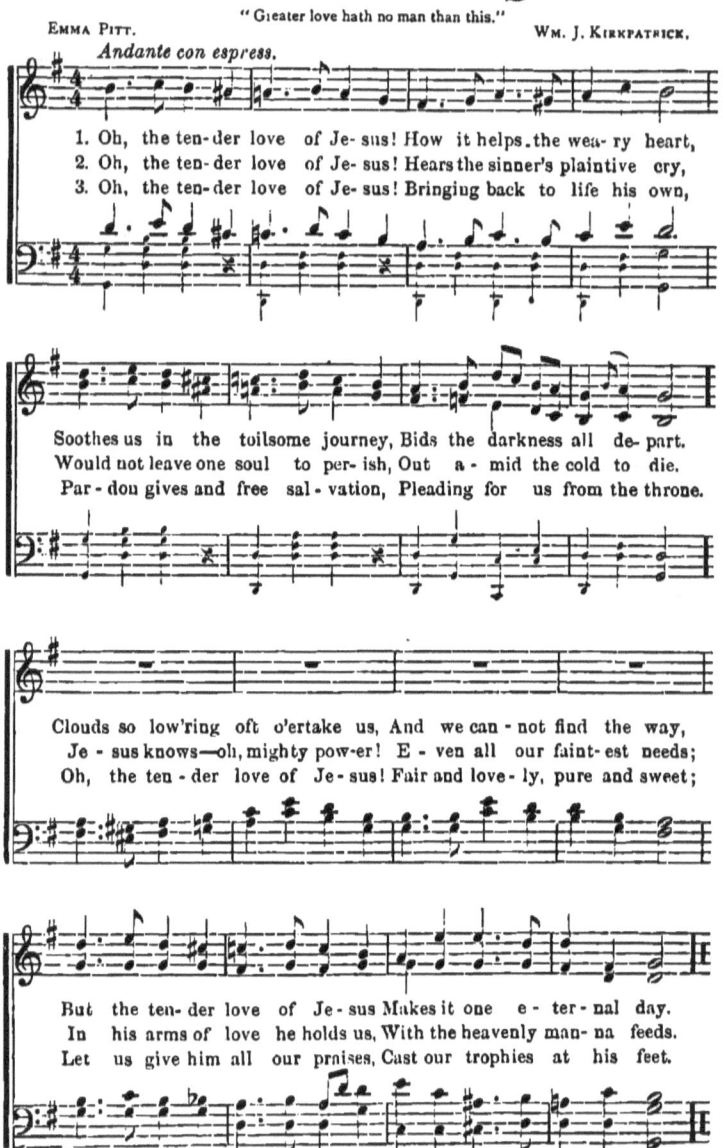

Here a Little, etc.—CONCLUDED.

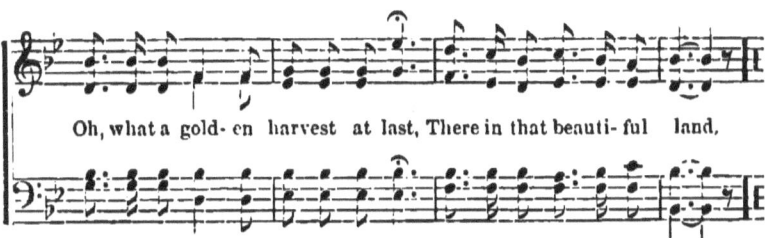

Oh, what a gold-en harvest at last, There in that beauti-ful land,

We'll Never be Afraid.

F. G. BURROUGHS. Cho. H. L. G. Ex. xiv: 13. H. L. GILMOUR.

1. Fear not the foe's advance, For thy salvation's near; Tho' mountains rise on either
2. Fear not, but forward go Into the waters deep, The waves shall part at his com-
3. Fear not if sorrow's flames A while thou must endure, For Christ will in the furnace
4. Fear not, for he hath said, Lo, I am always near, To strengthen, help, in all dis-

CHORUS.

side, God bids thee not to fear. We'll never be a-fraid, We'll never be a-
mand, The soul who trusts he'll keep.
be, And thou shalt come forth pure.
tress, And bids thee not to fear.

fraid, For the Saviour's form walks the wildest storm, We'll never be a-fraid.

Copyright, 1895, by H. L. Gilmour.

58. Jesus Will Welcome Me There.

Fanny J. Crosby.   Jno. R. Sweney.

1. Over the riv-er they call me, Friends that are dear to my heart;
2. Over the riv-er they call me, Hark, 'tis their voices I hear,
3. Over the riv-er, how love-ly, There is no sorrow nor night;
4. Over the riv-er they call me, Watching with glad, beaming eyes;

Soon shall I meet them in glo-ry, Never, no nev-er to part.
Borne on the wings of the twi-light, Murmuring soft-ly and clear.
There they are walking with Je-sus, Clothed in his garment of light.
O-ver the riv-er I'm com-ing, Joyful my spir-it re-plies.

CHORUS.

O-ver the riv-er to E-den, Home to their dwelling so fair;
An-gels will car-ry me safe-ly, Je-sus will welcome me there.

Copyright, 1892, by Jno. R. Sweney.

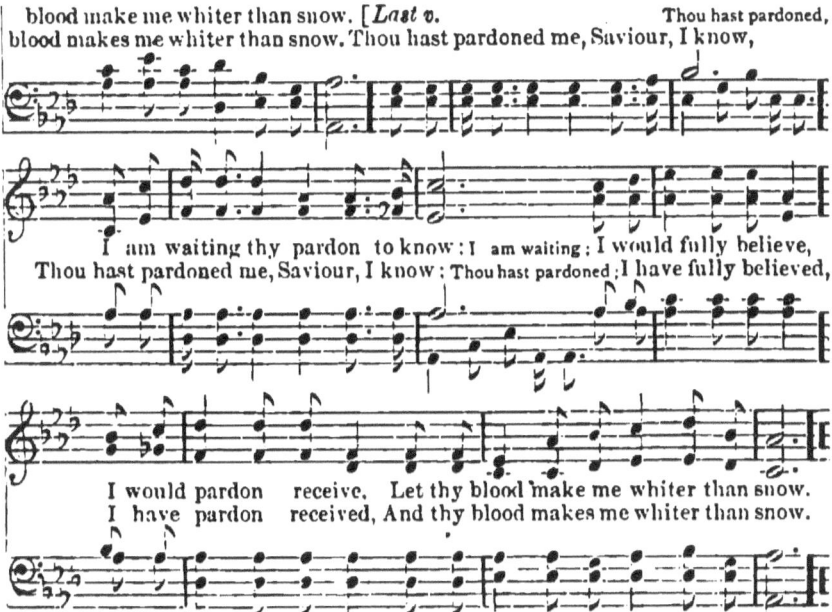

Sing and Rejoice.—CONCLUDED. 61

Use first four lines as Chorus. D.C.

bless- ings to show- er On ev- 'ry soul who will let Je- sus in.
those who are with us, Serv- ing him here till we're called to his feet.

We will Follow On.

E. R. LATTA.   WM. J. KIRKPATRICK.

1. Where the Saviour's hand is leading, We will fol- low, fol- low on;
2. Where the Saviour's voice is calling, We will fol- low, fol- low on;
3. In the way the star is showing, We will fol- low, fol- low on;
4. Still by faith our way pur- su- ing, We will fol- low, fol- low on;
5. 'Neath the cross to- geth- er banding, We will fol- low, fol- low on;

CHORUS.

His commands and warnings heeding, We will follow on. Follow on, follow on,
Show'rs of grace upon us falling, We will follow on.
To celestial mansions going, We will follow on.
Glad the land of promise viewing, We will follow on.
Ever toward the golden landing, We will follow on.

Till the heav'nly prize is won; Till we grasp a shining crown, Follow, follow on.

Copyright, 1892, by Wm. J. Kirkpatrick.

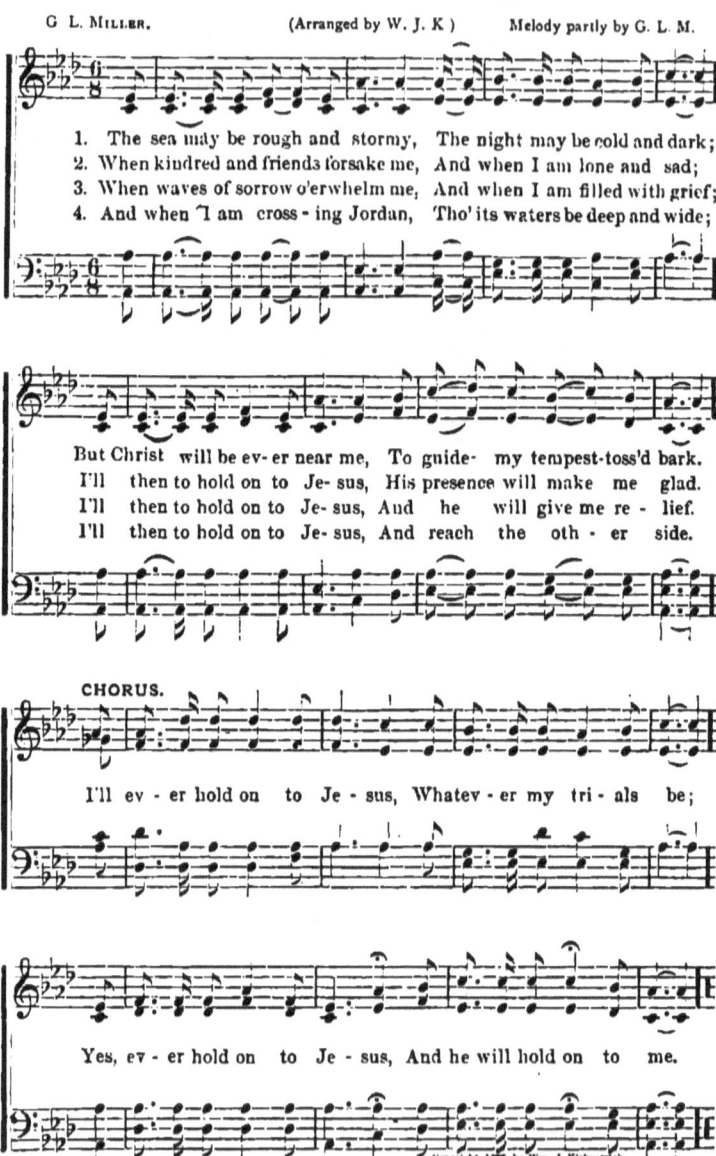

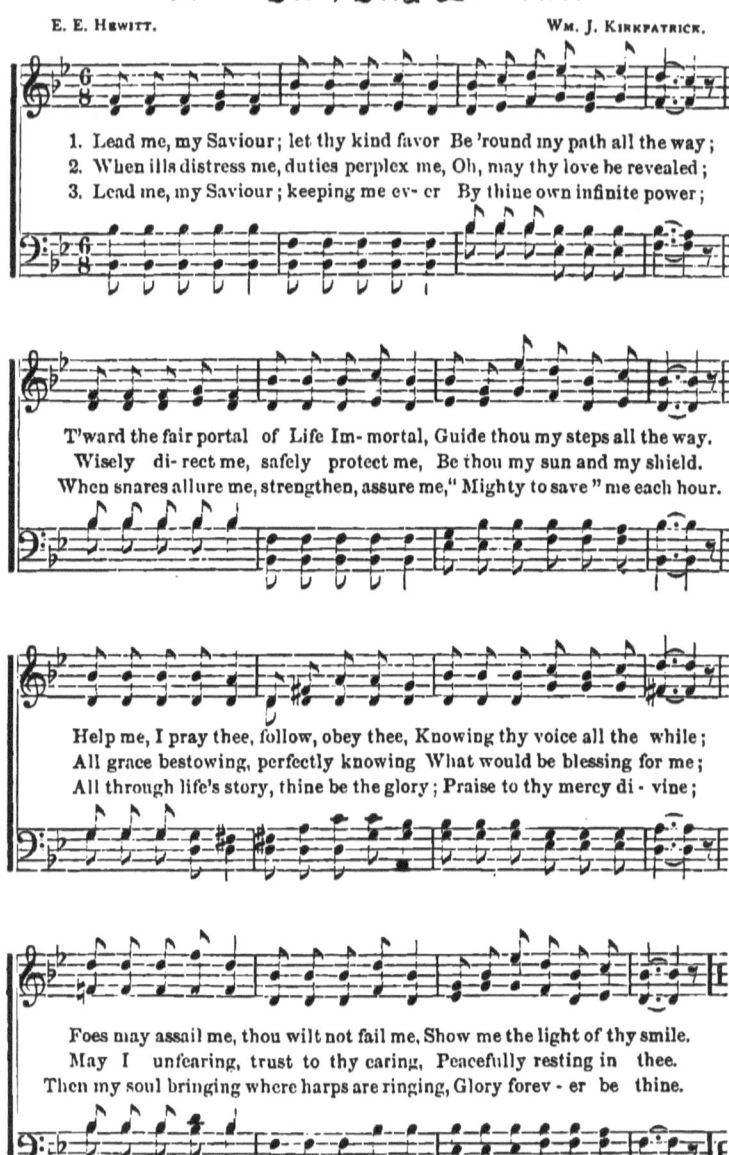

A Shelter in the Time of Storm. 65

"God is the rock of my refuge."—Ps. xciv: 22.

Words arranged.   A. J. Showalter. By per.

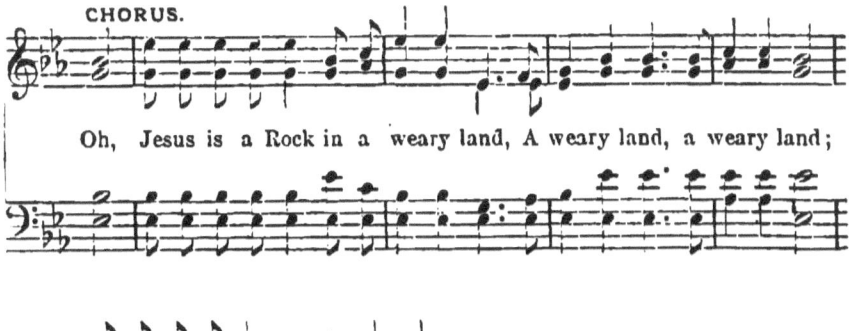

1. The Lord's our Rock, in him we hide, A shelter in the time of storm;
2. A shade by day, defence by night, A shelter in the time of storm;
3. The raging storms may round us beat, A shelter in the time of storm;
4. O Rock divine, O Refuge dear, A shelter in the time of storm;

Se- cure whatev - er may be- tide, A shelter in the time of storm.
No fears a- larm, no foes affright, A shelter in the time of storm.
We'll nev- er leave this safe retreat, A shelter in the time of storm.
Be thou our helper ev - er near, A shelter in the time of storm.

CHORUS.

Oh, Jesus is a Rock in a weary land, A weary land, a weary land;

Jesus is a Rock in a weary land, A shelter in the time of storm.

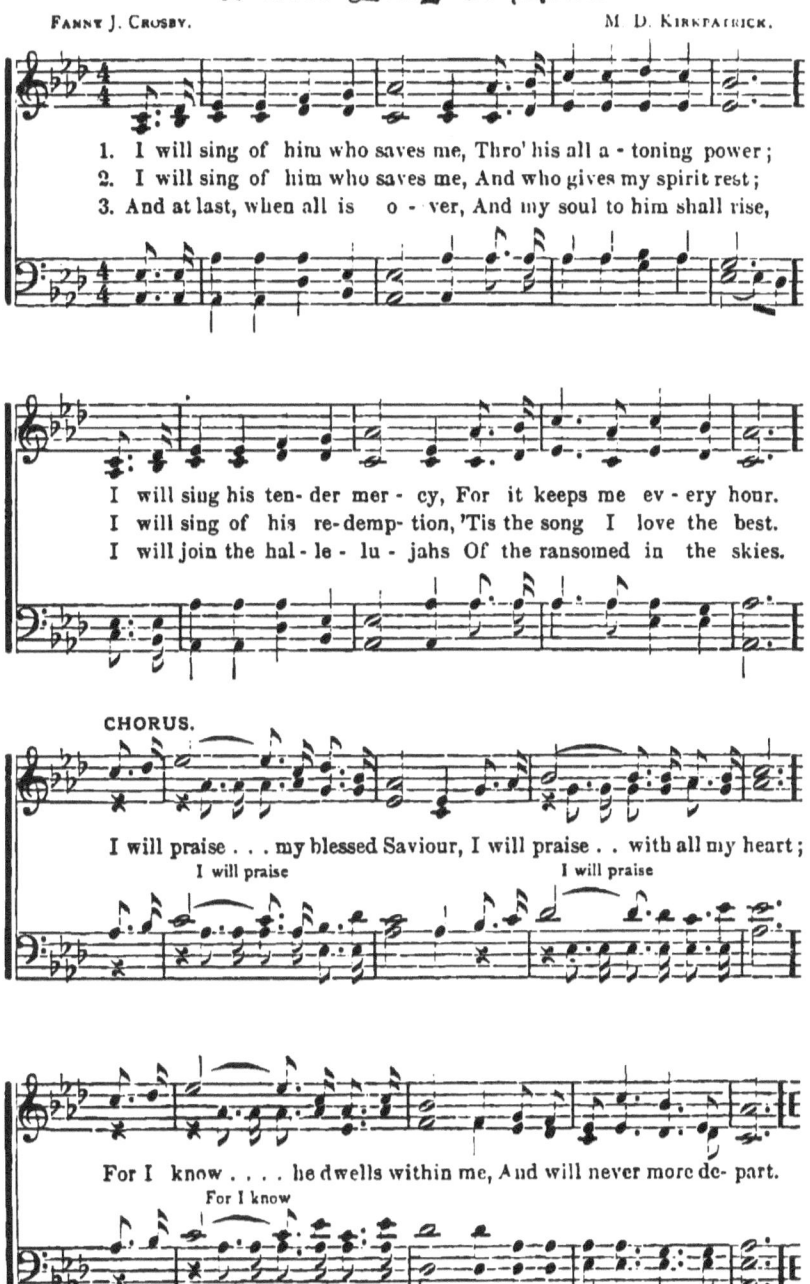

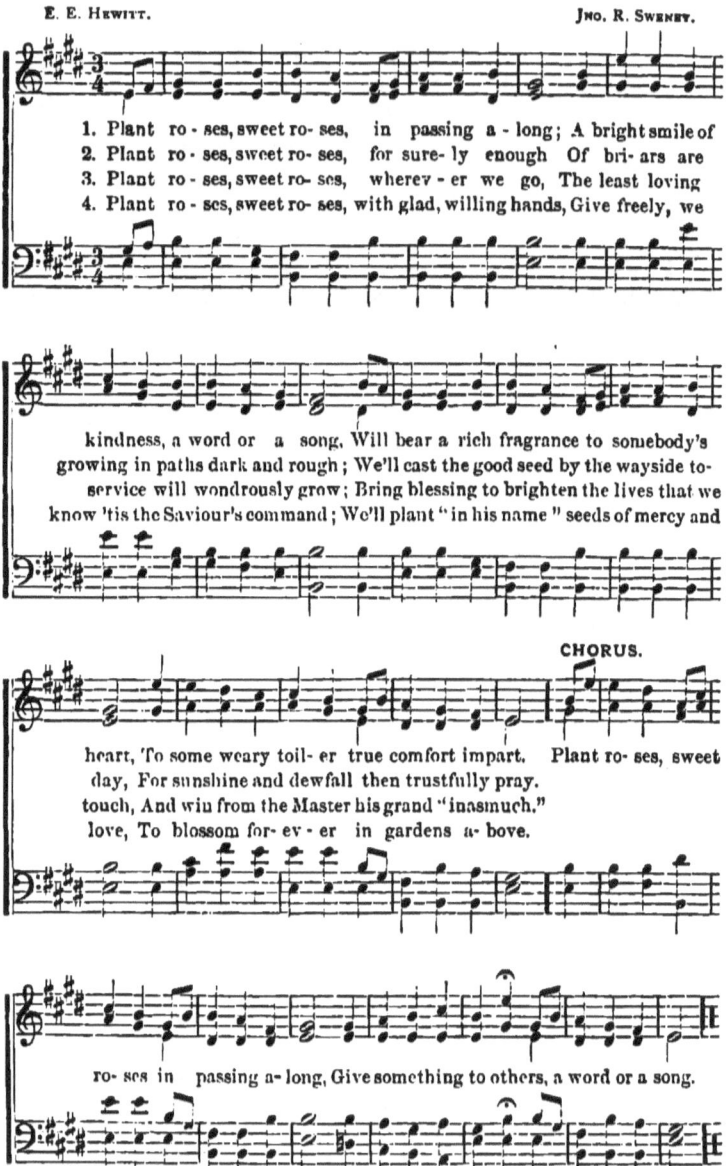

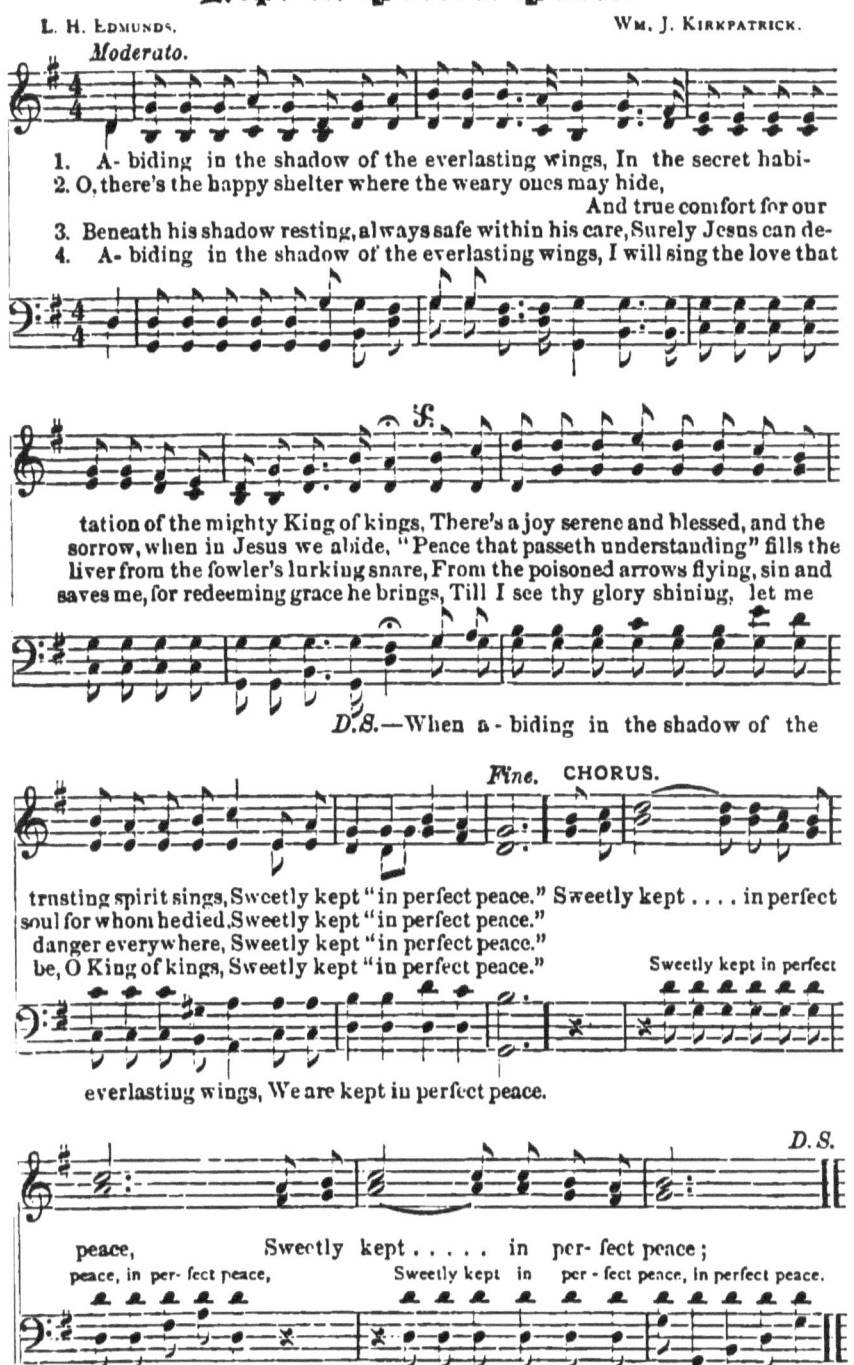

Rejoicing Evermore.—CONCLUDED.

joic- ing ev - ermore, Un- til we sing for-ev - er on the shining shore.

Lord, have Mercy.

S. P. M. Wm. J. Kirkpatrick.

Very slow.

1. Lord, have mercy, oh, have mercy, Lord, have mercy, hear my cry;
2. May thy Spirit, Ho - ly Spir- it, May thy Spirit make me whole;
3. While I'm pleading, humbly pleading, While I'm pleading, hear my call;
4. Now I'm trusting, sweetly trusting, Trusting in thy mighty power;

Saviour, help me, come, and help me, Saviour, help me, or I die.
Send sal- va- tion, full sal- va- tion, Send sal- va- tion to my soul.
Let thy blessing, promised blessing, Let thy blessing on me fall.
Saviour, keep me, ev - er keep me, Saviour, keep me from this hour.

CHORUS. *Repeat pp.*

Lord, have mercy, oh, have mercy, Lord, have mercy on my soul.

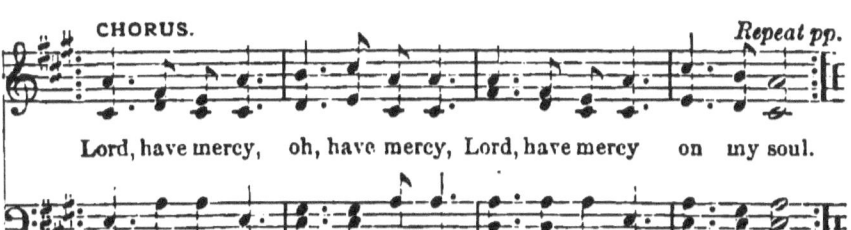

Copyright, 1892, by Wm. J. Kirkpatrick.

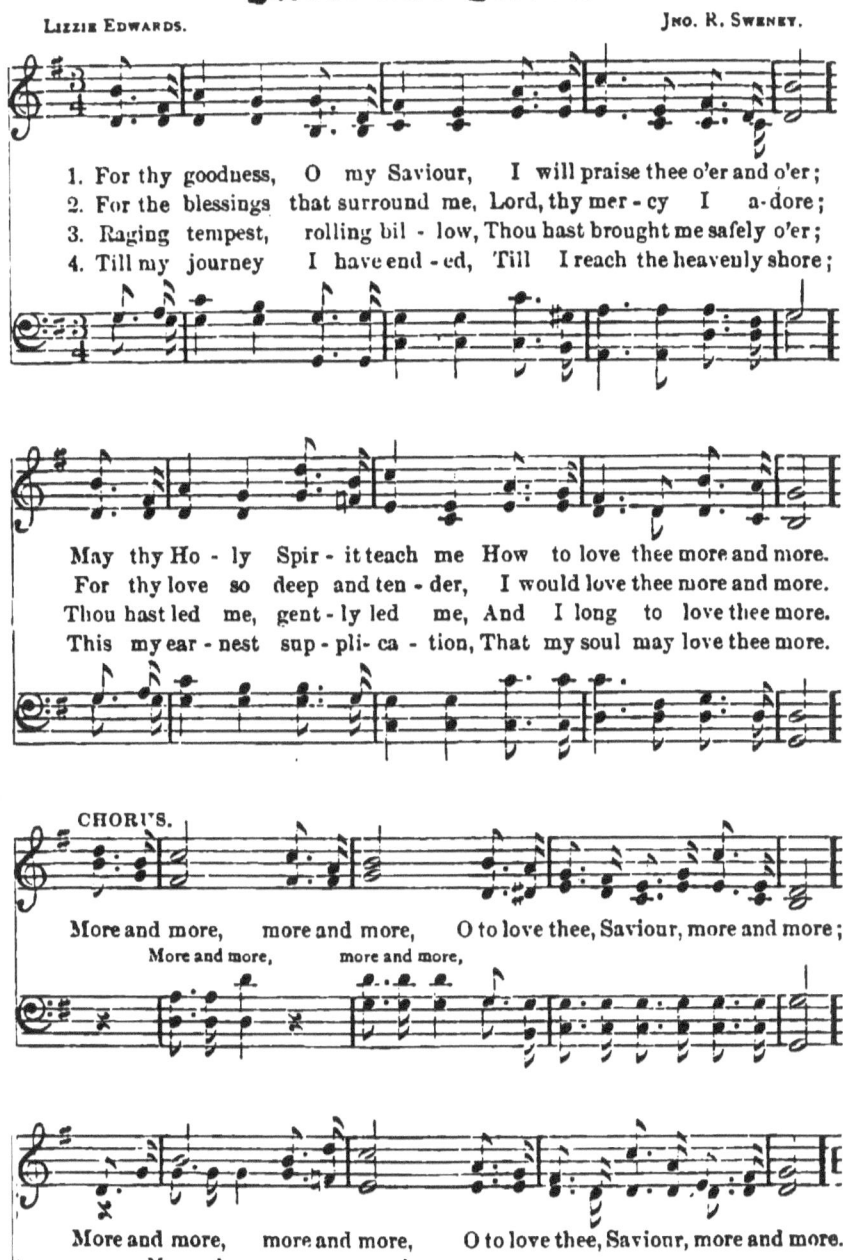

On the Jericho Road.—CONCLUDED. 75

Tell him of a Saviour's wondrous love, Tell him of a home prepared a-bove.

The Fold of Love.

ABBIE MILLS.   Ezek. xxxiv: 14.   H. L. GILMOUR.

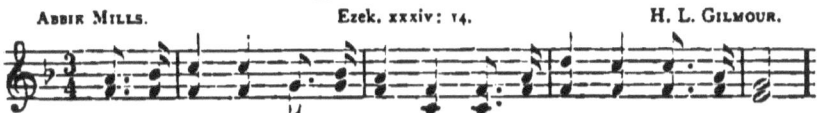

1. I am feeding on the mountains, Resting in the fold of love,
2. Je-sus bought me, Jesus sought me, In a dark and cloud-y day;
3. To my heart, all wea-ry, broken, Swift he came with precious balm;
4. While I sing of cleansing, healing, How the waves of mu-sic roll!
5. Oh, the ful-ness of salvation, Streaming brooks these mountains know!

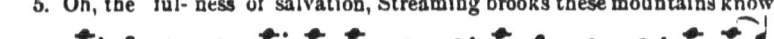

Close beside the liv-ing fountains, Flowing from the throne a-bove.
From the des-ert wastes he brought me, In the land of corn to stay.
Oh, how sweet the Spir-it's to-ken, Sing, my soul, the endless psalm!
Sweet the hal-le-lu-jahs, stealing O'er each chord within my soul.
Here is flow-ing God's li-ba-tion, Making sin-ners white as snow.

D.S.—Yes. I'm in green pastures feed-ing, Resting in the fold of love.

CHORUS.   *D.S.*

Hal-le-lu-jah! now he fills me, Ho-ly Spir-it, Heavenly Dove;

Copyright, 1895, by H. L. Gilmour.

6 Onward still my Shepherd calls me,
  Where the healthful morsels lie;
So, I know whate'er befalls me,
  He will all my need supply.

7 Fed in pastures, bathed in glory
  From the palaces on high;
I am shouting back the story,
  That the upper fold is nigh.

The Simple, Earnest Prayer.

Fanny J. Crosby.   Jno. R. Sweney.

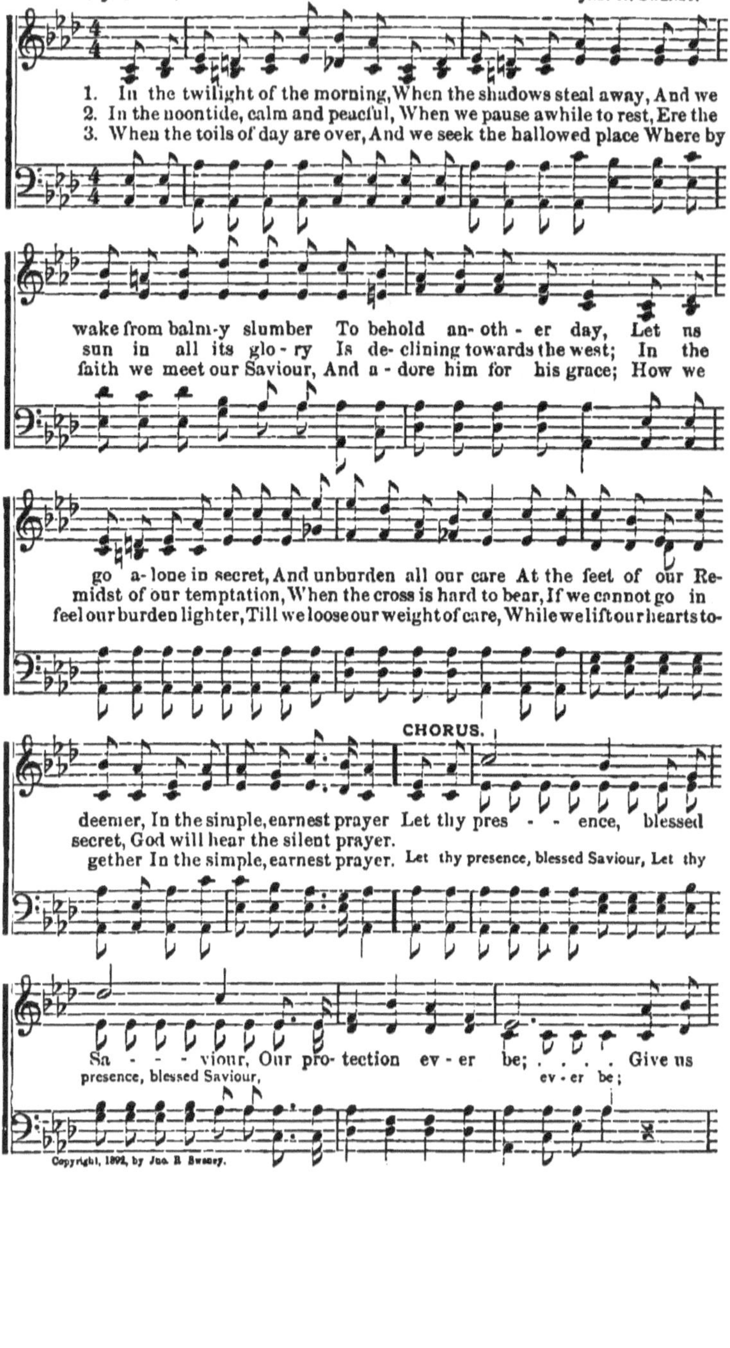

1. In the twilight of the morning, When the shadows steal away, And we wake from balm-y slumber To behold an-oth-er day, Let us go a-lone in secret, And unburden all our care At the feet of our Redeemer, In the simple, earnest prayer.
2. In the noontide, calm and peaceful, When we pause awhile to rest, Ere the sun in all its glo-ry Is de-clining towards the west; In the midst of our temptation, When the cross is hard to bear, If we cannot go in secret, God will hear the silent prayer.
3. When the toils of day are over, And we seek the hallowed place Where by faith we meet our Saviour, And a-dore him for his grace; How we feel our burden lighter, Till we loose our weight of care, While we lift our hearts to-gether In the simple, earnest prayer.

CHORUS.

Let thy presence, blessed Saviour, Our pro-tection ev-er be; Give us...

Copyright, 1892, by Jno. R. Sweney.

The Simple, Earnest Prayer.—CONCLUDED. 77

strength for ev-'ry tri - - al, Keep, oh, keep us close to thee.
Give us strength   for ev'ry tri-al,

He's with Me all the Time.

M. D. K.   M. D. KIRKPATRICK.

1. My soul is full of gladness, My heart is full of song; My loving Friend, my
2. I hold the hand of Jesus, He keeps me safe alway; Thro' unknown paths he
3. I walk in brightest sunshine, That shines along the way, It is the smile of
4. I hear the softest mu-sic, Like bells of silver chime, It is the voice of

CHORUS.

Je-sus, Is with me all day long. He's with me all the day, He's
guides me, He's with me all the day.
Je-sus, He's with me all the day.
Je-sus, He's with me all the time.

with me all the time ; My loving Friend, my Jesus, He's with me all the time.

Copyright, 1892, by Wm. J. Kirkpatrick.

78. Jesus the Children's Friend.

W. L. M.
W. L. Mason.

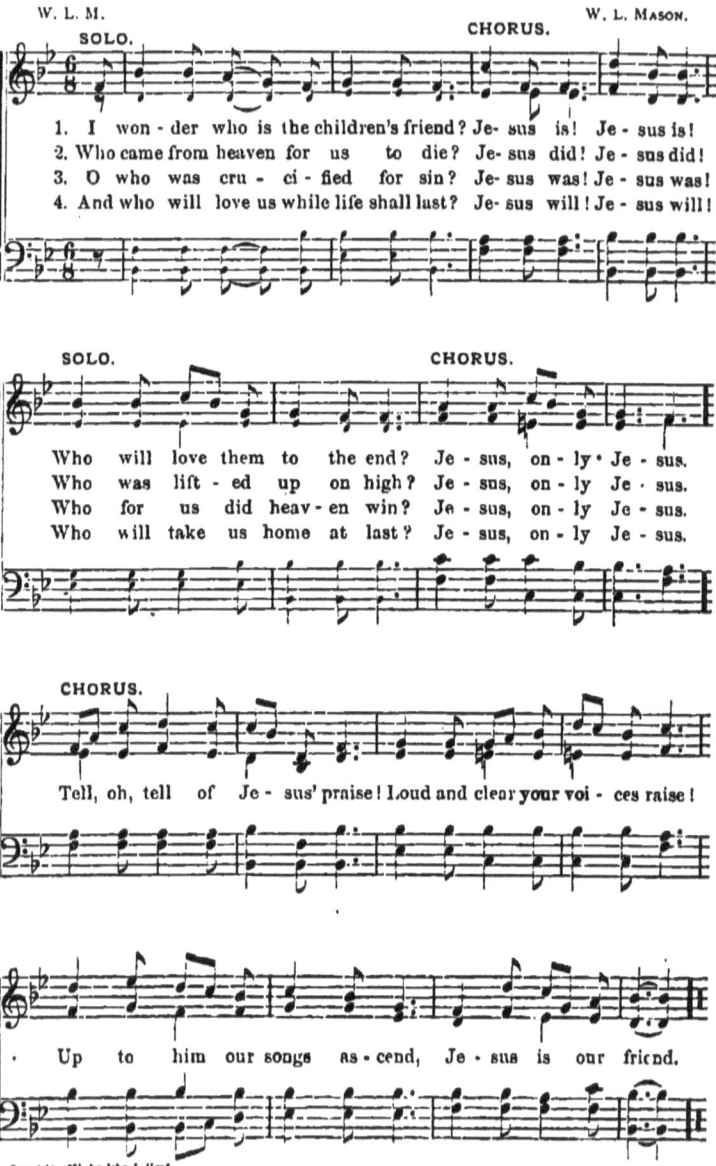

1. I won-der who is the children's friend? Je- sus is! Je- sus is!
2. Who came from heaven for us to die? Je- sus did! Je- sus did!
3. O who was cru - ci - fied for sin? Je- sus was! Je- sus was!
4. And who will love us while life shall last? Je- sus will! Je- sus will!

Who will love them to the end? Je - sus, on - ly Je - sus.
Who was lift - ed up on high? Je - sus, on - ly Je - sus.
Who for us did heav - en win? Je - sus, on - ly Je - sus.
Who will take us home at last? Je - sus, on - ly Je - sus.

Tell, oh, tell of Je - sus' praise! Loud and clear your voi - ces raise!

Up to him our songs as - cend, Je - sus is our friend.

Copyright, 1891, by John J. Hood.

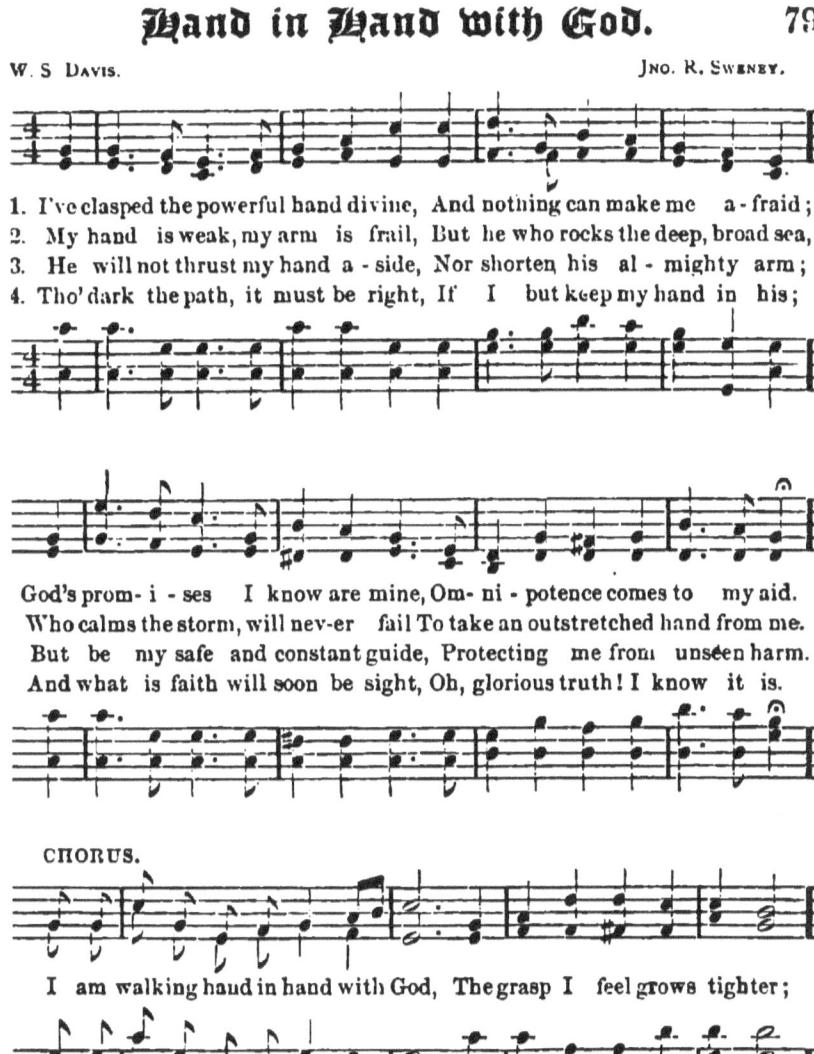

We are Nearing. 81

FANNY J. CROSBY. JNO. R. SWENEY.

1. We are drifting towards the waters Of a calm and tranquil sea,
2. We are drifting from the sorrows That for us will soon be o'er;
3. We are drifting from the shadows In - to pure and perfect day;
4. Oh, the morning and the meeting, When our happy souls shall rest,

And we soon shall anchor safe - ly In that port where we would be.
We are drifting from the tri - als That will vex the heart no more.
'Tis the Saviour guides our ves- sel, And his presence cheers our way.
By the fount of life e - ter - nal, With the ransomed ev - er blest.

CHORUS.

We are near - ing, we are near - ing, Nearing the golden strand;
We are nearing, nearing, we are nearing, nearing,

We are near - ing, we are near - ing, Nearing the soul's bright land.

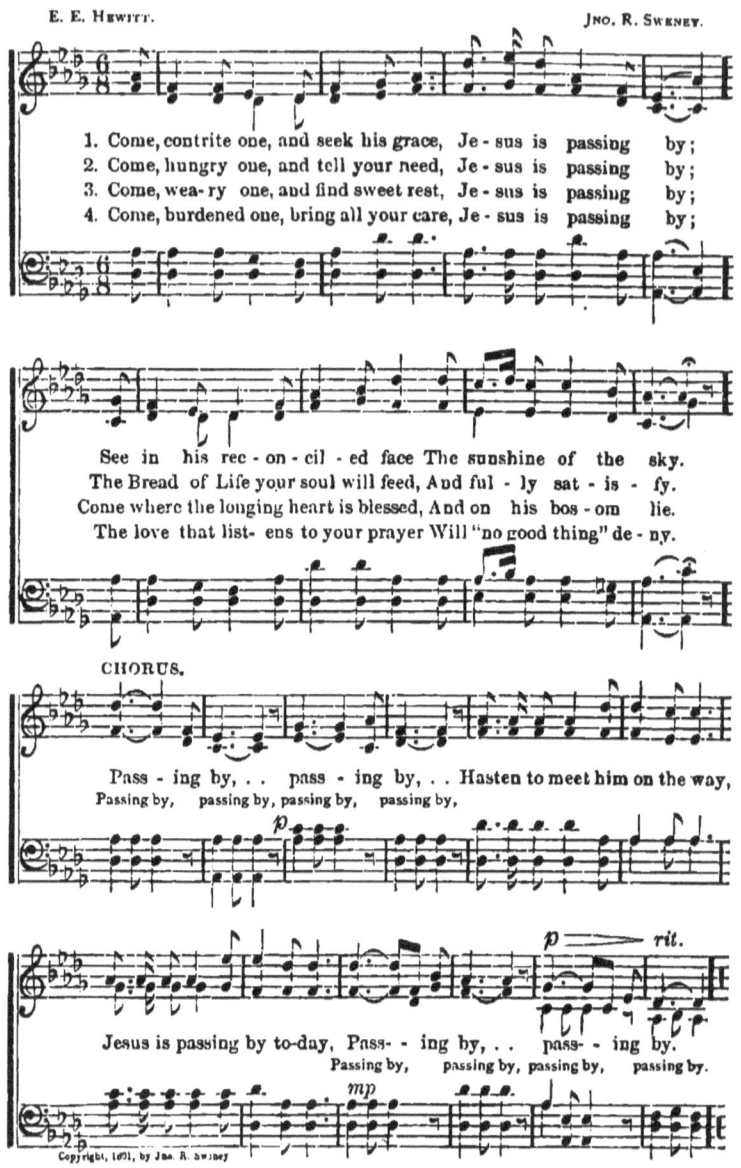

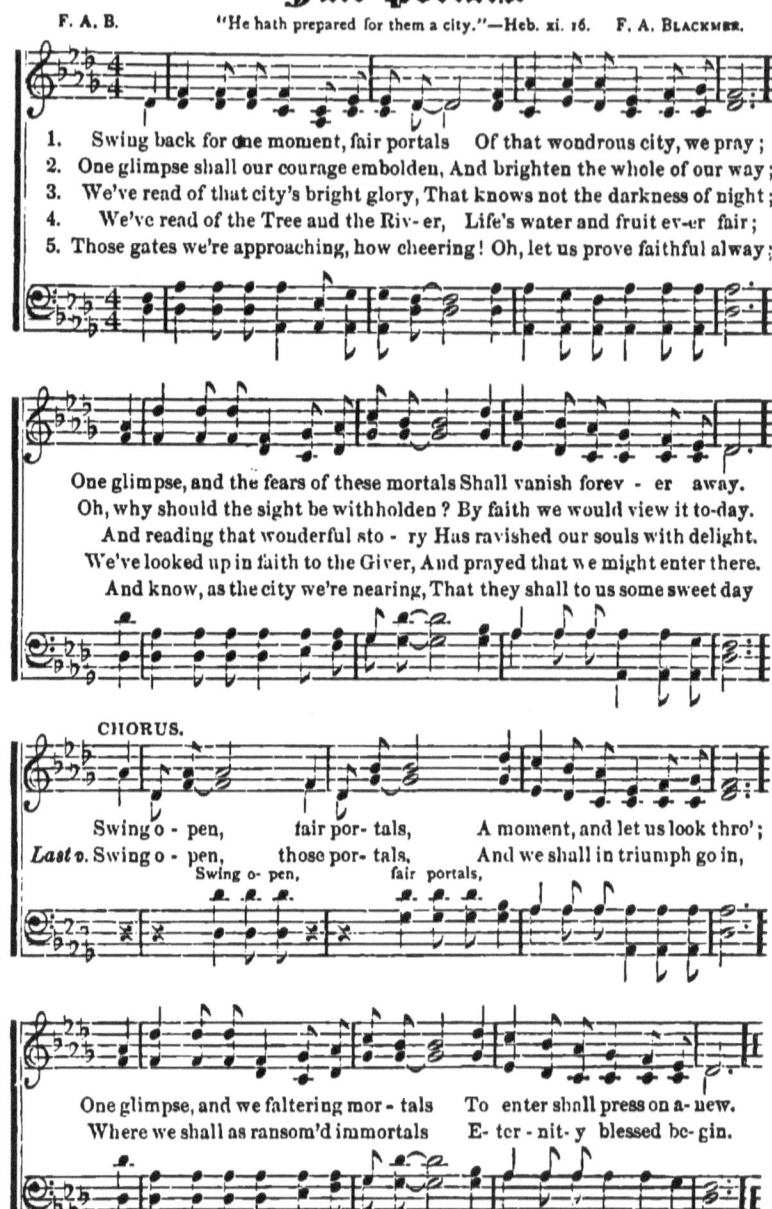

Watch and Pray. 87

FANNY J. CROSBY. WM. J. KIRKPATRICK.

1. Watch and pray that when the Master cometh, If at morning, noon or night,
2. Watch and pray; the tempter may be near us; Keep the heart with jealous care,
3. Watch and pray, nor let us ev-er wea-ry; Jesus watched and prayed alone:
4. Watch and pray, nor leave our post of duty, Till we hear the Bridegroom's voice:

He may find a lamp in ev'ry window, Trimmed and burning clear and bright.
Lest the door, a moment left unguard-ed, Evil thoughts may enter there.
Prayed for us when on-ly stars beheld him, While on Olive's brow they shone.
Then, with him the marriage feast partaking, We shall ev-ermore re-joice.

CHORUS.

Watch and pray, ... the Lord command - - - eth; Watch and
Watch and pray, the Lord commandeth, Watch and pray, the Lord commandeth; Watch and

pray, ... 'twill not be long: Soon he'll gath - - -
pray, 'twill not be long, Watch and pray, 'twill not be long: Soon he'll gather home his

- - - er home his loved ones To the happy vale of song. of song.
loved ones, Soon he'll gather home his loved ones To the happy vale of song. the vale of song.

Copyright, 1886, by Wm. J. Kirkpatrick.

88. Resting, Sweetly Resting.

L. H. Edmunds.   Wm. J. Kirkpatrick.

Moderato.

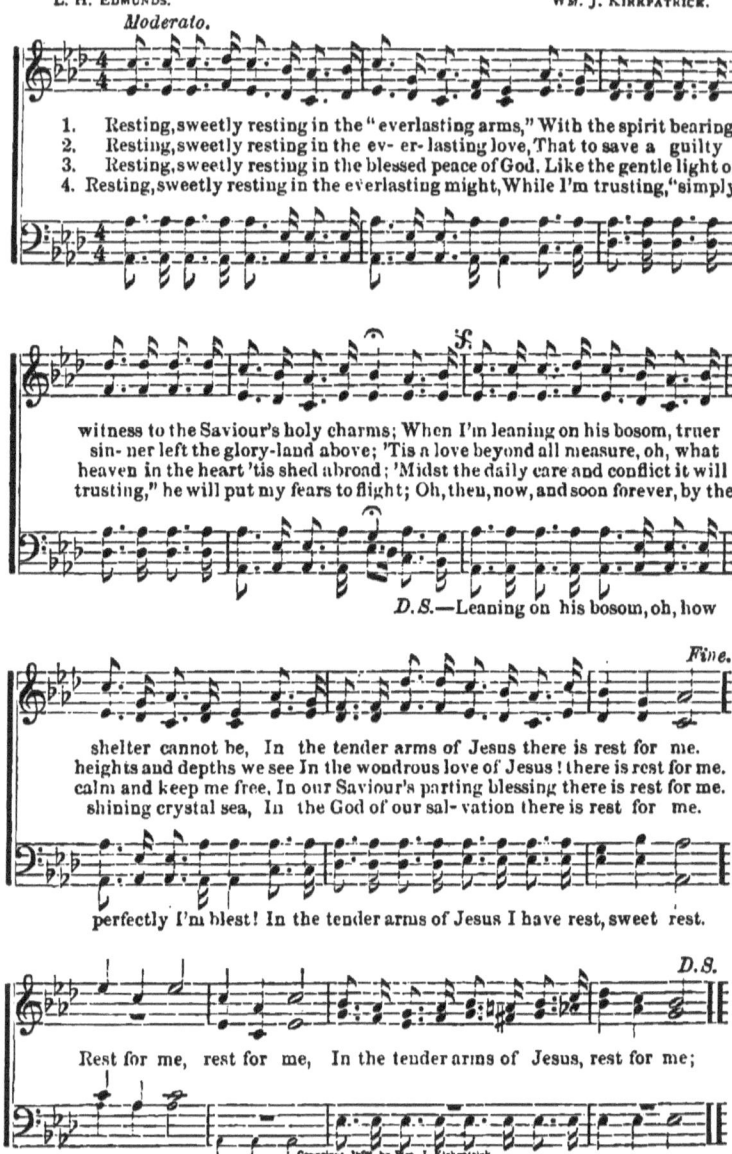

1. Resting, sweetly resting in the "everlasting arms," With the spirit bearing
2. Resting, sweetly resting in the ev- er- lasting love, That to save a guilty
3. Resting, sweetly resting in the blessed peace of God, Like the gentle light of
4. Resting, sweetly resting in the everlasting might, While I'm trusting, "simply

witness to the Saviour's holy charms; When I'm leaning on his bosom, truer
sin- ner left the glory-land above; 'Tis a love beyond all measure, oh, what
heaven in the heart 'tis shed abroad; 'Midst the daily care and conflict it will
trusting," he will put my fears to flight; Oh, then, now, and soon forever, by the

D.S.—Leaning on his bosom, oh, how

shelter cannot be, In the tender arms of Jesus there is rest for me.
heights and depths we see In the wondrous love of Jesus! there is rest for me.
calm and keep me free, In our Saviour's parting blessing there is rest for me.
shining crystal sea, In the God of our sal- vation there is rest for me.

perfectly I'm blest! In the tender arms of Jesus I have rest, sweet rest.

Rest for me, rest for me, In the tender arms of Jesus, rest for me;

Copyright, 1892, by Wm. J. Kirkpatrick.

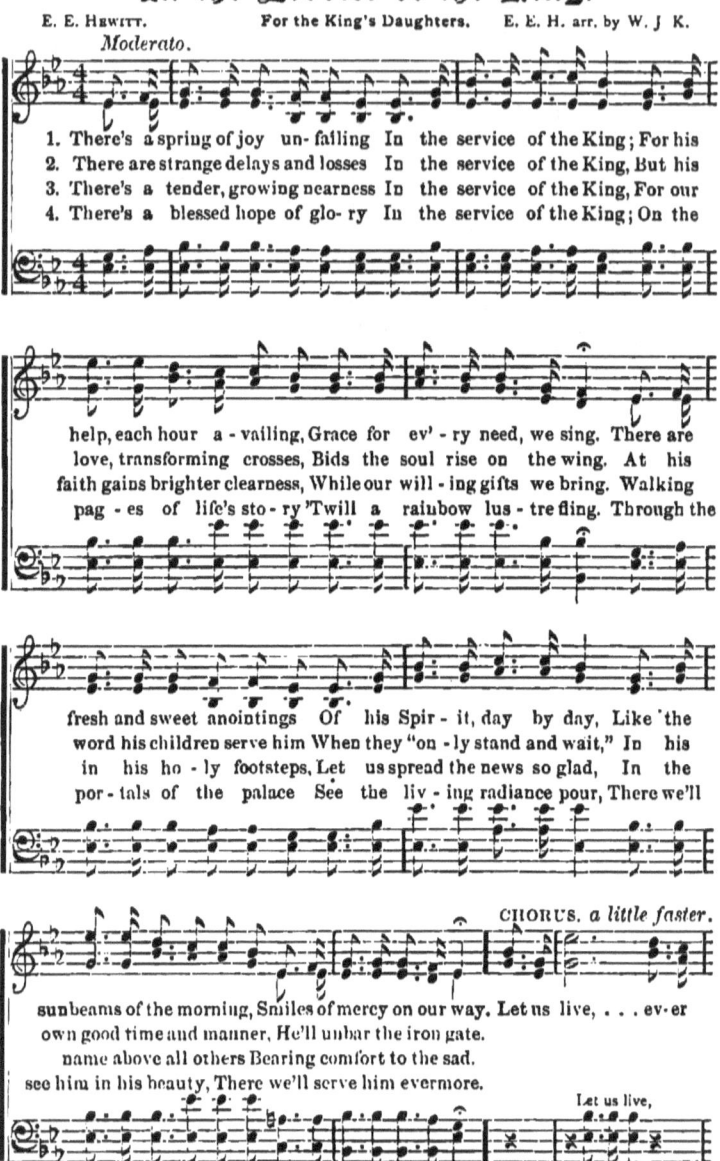

In the Service of the King.—CONCLUDED. 91

Follow All the Way.

Geo. W. Collins. Arr. by W. J. K.

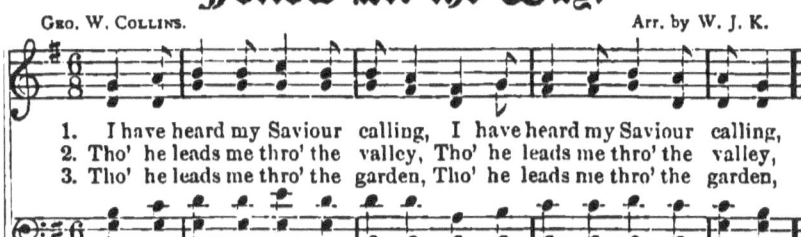

1. I have heard my Saviour calling, I have heard my Saviour calling,
2. Tho' he leads me thro' the valley, Tho' he leads me thro' the valley,
3. Tho' he leads me thro' the garden, Tho' he leads me thro' the garden,

Cho.—Where he leads me I will follow, Where he leads me I will follow,

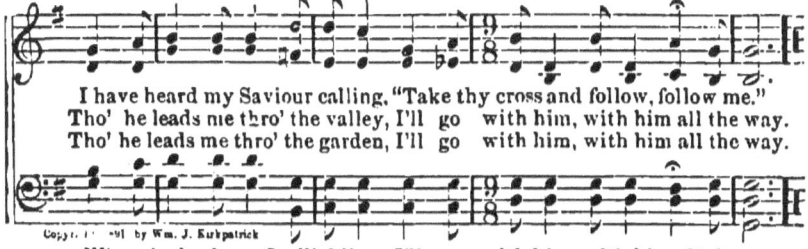

I have heard my Saviour calling, "Take thy cross and follow, follow me."
Tho' he leads me thro' the valley, I'll go with him, with him all the way.
Tho' he leads me thro' the garden, I'll go with him, with him all the way.

Copyright, 1891, by Wm. J. Kirkpatrick.

Where he leads me I will follow, I'll go with him, with him all the way.

4 ‖: Tho' the path be dark and dreary, :‖
   I'll go with him, with him all the way.
5 ‖: Tho' he leads me to the conflict, :‖
   I'll go with him, with him all the way.
6 ‖: Tho' he leads through fiery trials, :‖
   I'll go with him, with him all the way.

7 ‖: I will follow on to know him :‖
   He's my Saviour, Saviour, Brother, Friend.
8 ‖: He will give me grace and glory, :‖
   He will keep me, keep me all the way.
9 ‖: O 'tis sweet to follow Jesus, :‖
   And be with him, with him all the way.

94. Happy in a Saviour's Love.

HENRIETTA E. BLAIR. WM. J. KIRKPATRICK.

1. While we walk by faith in the King's highway, Happy in a Saviour's love;
2. Tho' the clouds may form and the storms may fall, Happy in a Saviour's love;
3. O the peace that dwells in a trusting soul, Happy in a Saviour's love;
4. We are going home from a world of care, Happy in a Saviour's love;

We will work and sing, we will watch and pray, Happy in a Saviour's love.
With a firm, strong hope we may leave them all, Happy in a Saviour's love.
We can shout for joy, tho' the waves may roll, Happy in a Saviour's love.
By the grace of God we shall soon be there, Happy in a Saviour's love.

CHORUS.

In a Sa - - viour's love, In a Sa - - viour's love;
In a Saviour's love, In a Saviour's love, Happy in a Saviour's love;

We will work and sing, we will watch and pray, Happy in a Saviour's love.

Copyright, 1892, by Wm. J. Kirkpatrick.

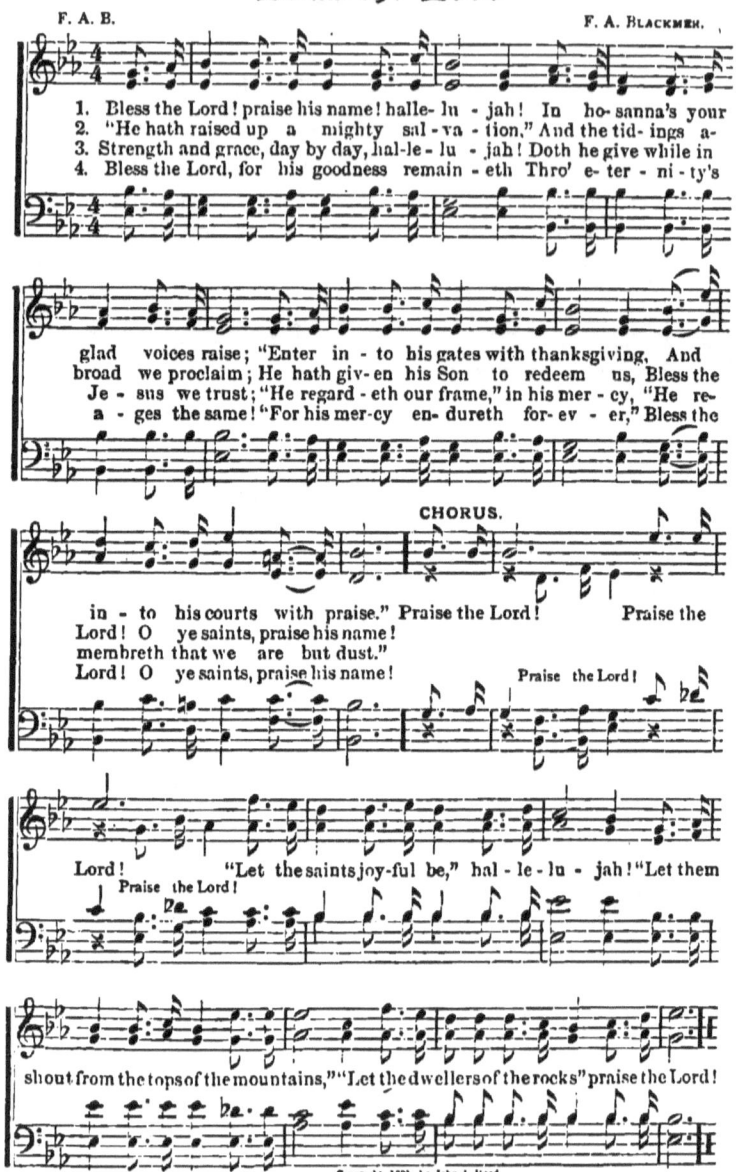

old corn of Canaan before me is spread, In Je - sus my joy is complete.

I Shall be Satisfied.

Bonar.
Moderato.

Rev. T. C. Neal.

1. When I shall wake in that fair morn of morns, Af - ter whose dawning
2. When I shall see thy glo- ry face to face, When in thine arms thou
3. When I shall meet with those that I have loved, Clasp in my eag - er
4. When I shall gaze up - on the face of him Who for me died, with

never night returns, And with whose glory day eternal burns, I shall be satis- fied.
wilt thy child embrace, When thou shalt open all thy stores of grace, I shall be satisfied.
arms the long removed, And find how faithful thou to me hast proved, I shall be satisfied.
eye no longer dim, And praise him with the everlasting hymn, I shall be satisfied.

CHORUS.   *rit.*

I shall be satisfied, I shall be satisfied, I shall be sat-is-fied, By and by.

From "Jasper and Gold," by per.

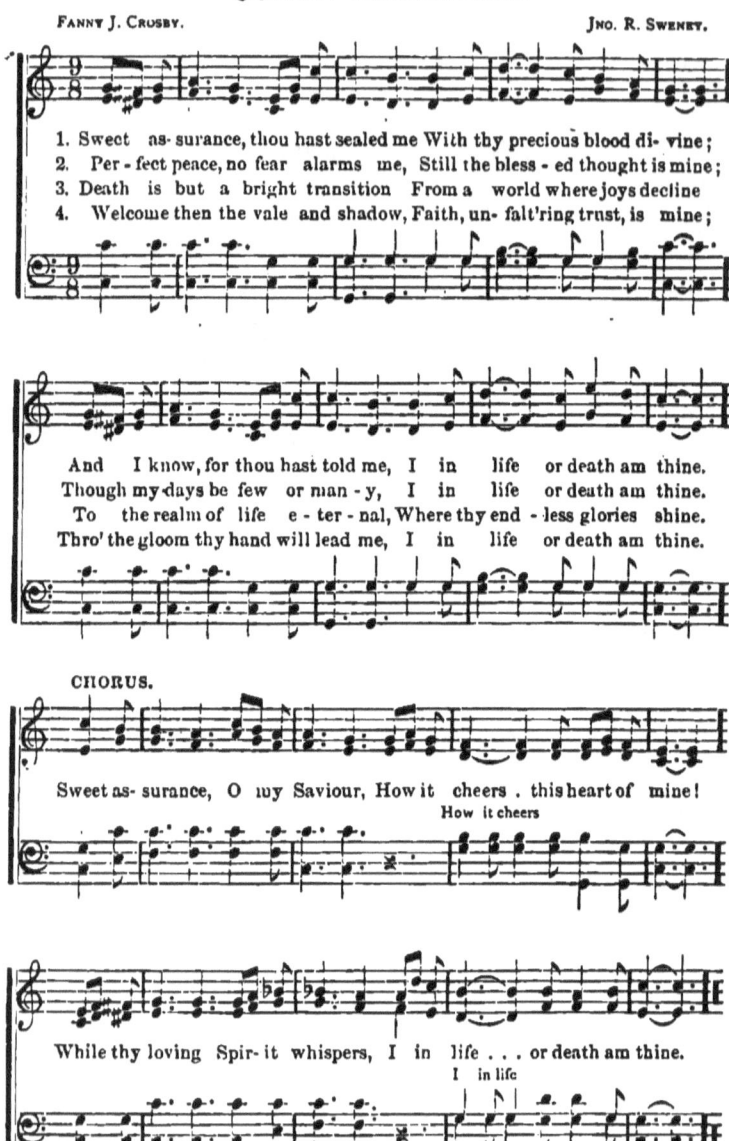

Be not Afraid; 'tis I. 103

WM. BRANDLE.   H. L. GILMOUR.

1. How sweet 'twould be when on life's sea, A - mid the tempest roar,
2. Then all a-glow to see and know Our Sa-viour at our side,
3. And does he not thus speak to us? Yes, when we read his word,
4. O Sa-viour, we would worthy be Of thine a-bode of love,

When straining eyes meet sea and skies, But not the dis-tant shore,
With strength renewed thro' tempest rude We'd to our ha - ven glide;
In ev - 'ry line that voice divine The ear of faith has heard,
And lost in joy, our notes employ With all the choirs a-bove;

To see our Saviour's gracious form, And hear his cheering cry,
Though death our fee-ble bark destroys We would not fear to die,
Still call-ing us to lean on him Who is for ev - er nigh,
When friends re-linquish us with tears We'll yield without a sigh,

A - mid the rag- ing of the storm,"Be not afraid; 'tis I."
Could we but hear that gen-tle voice, "Be not afraid; 'tis I."
To whis- per in the darkness grim,"Be not afraid; 'tis I."

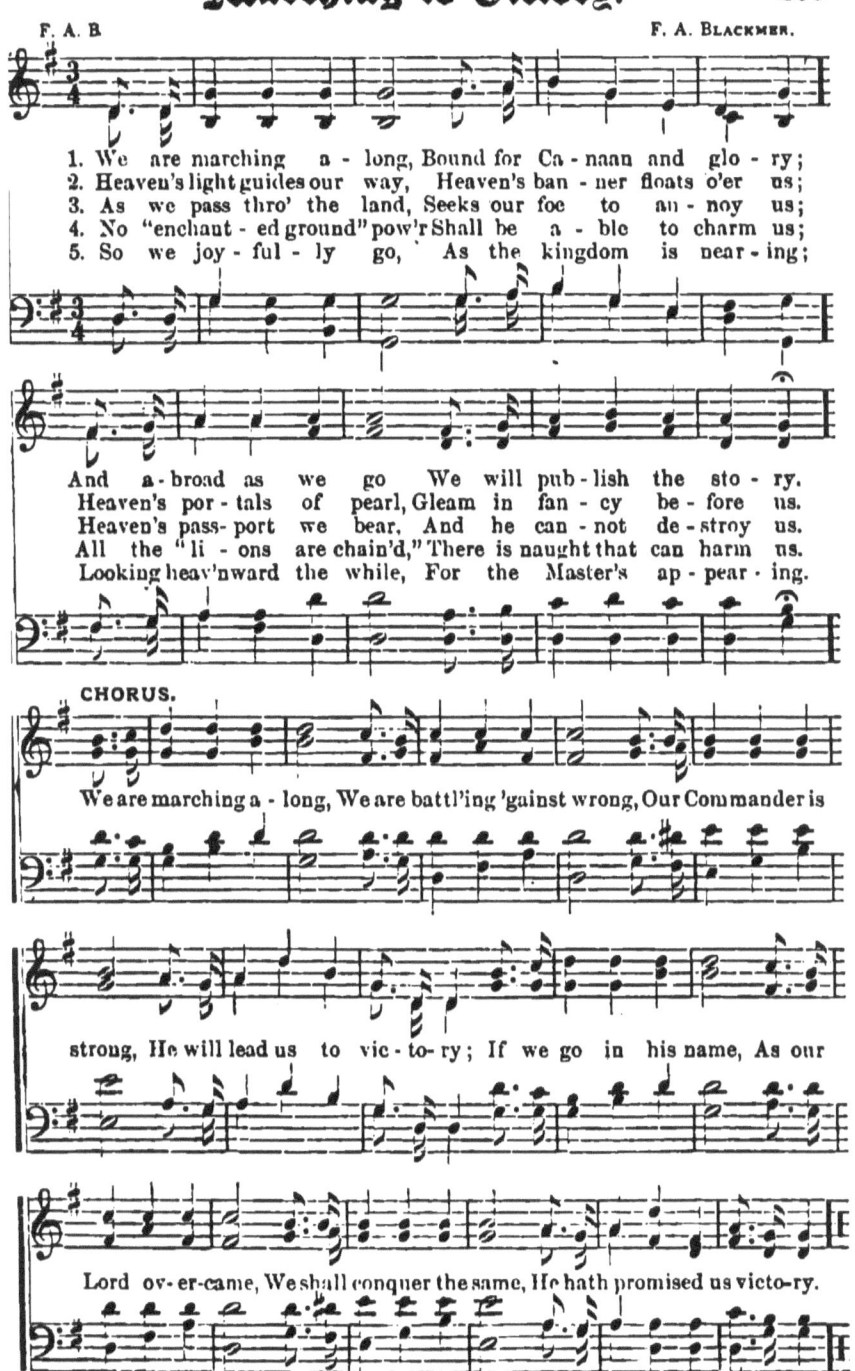

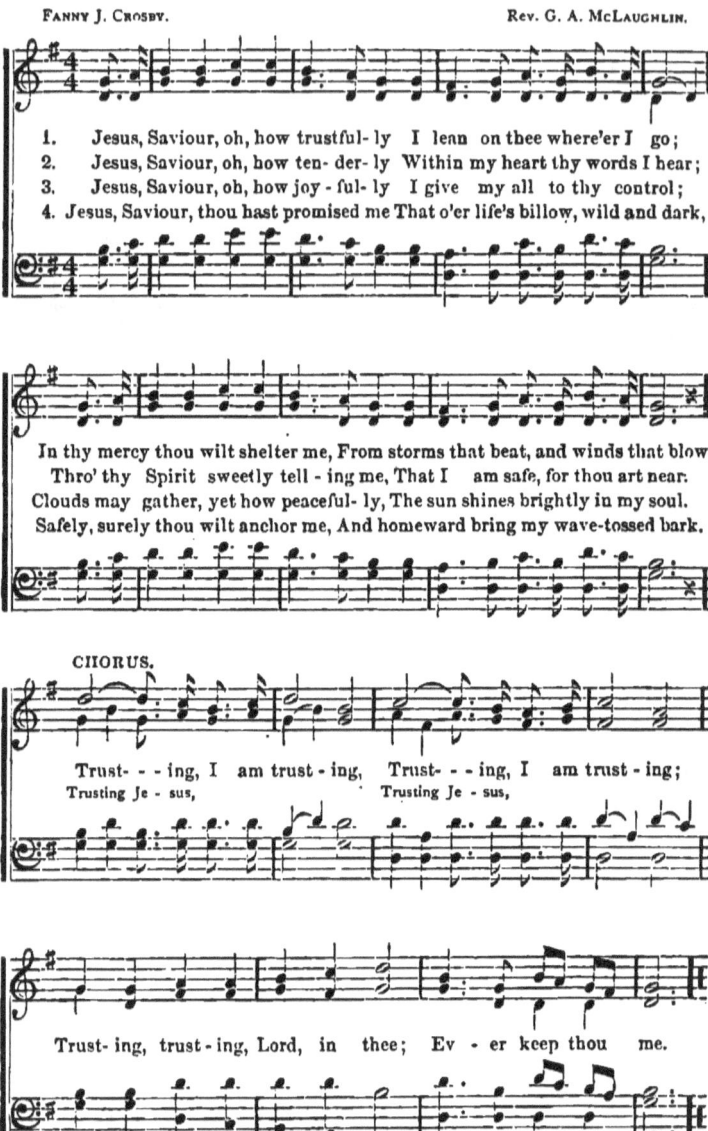

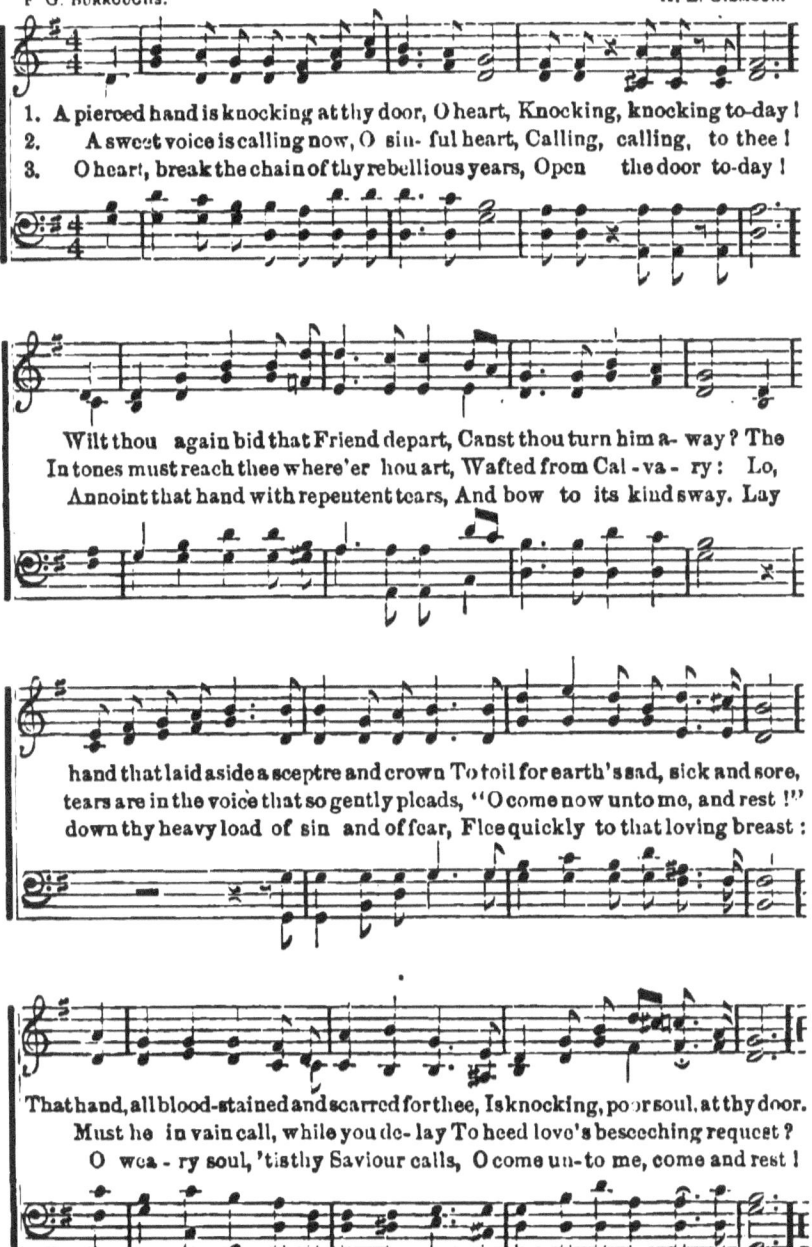

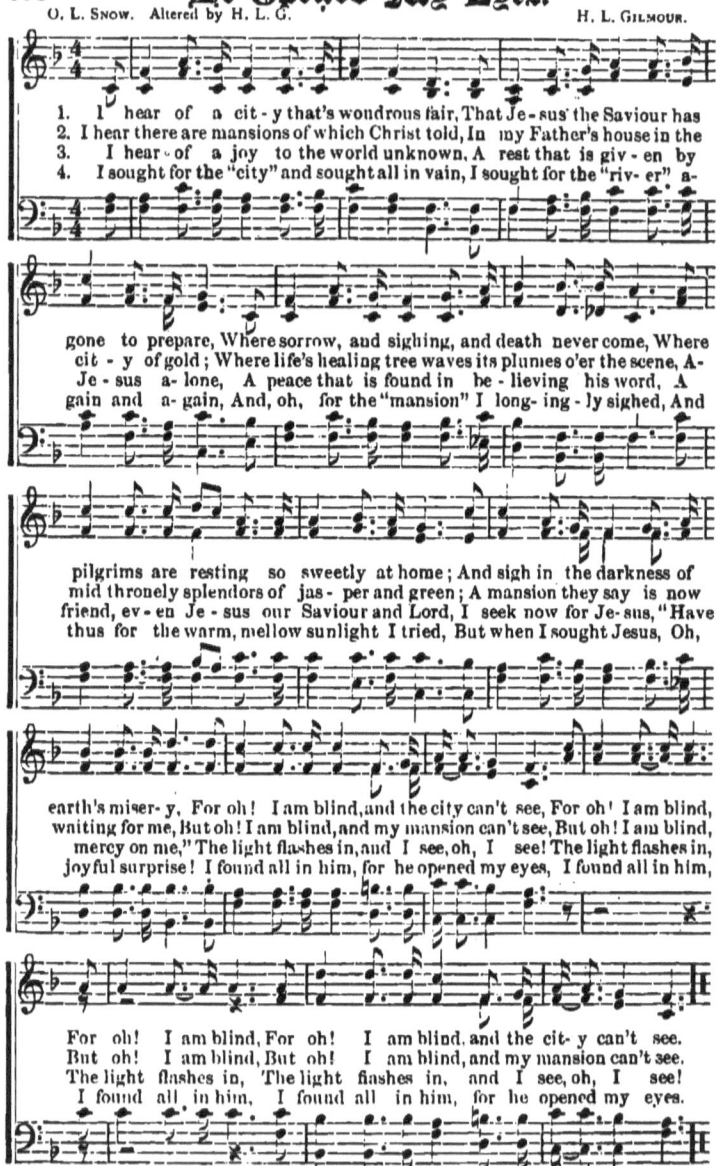

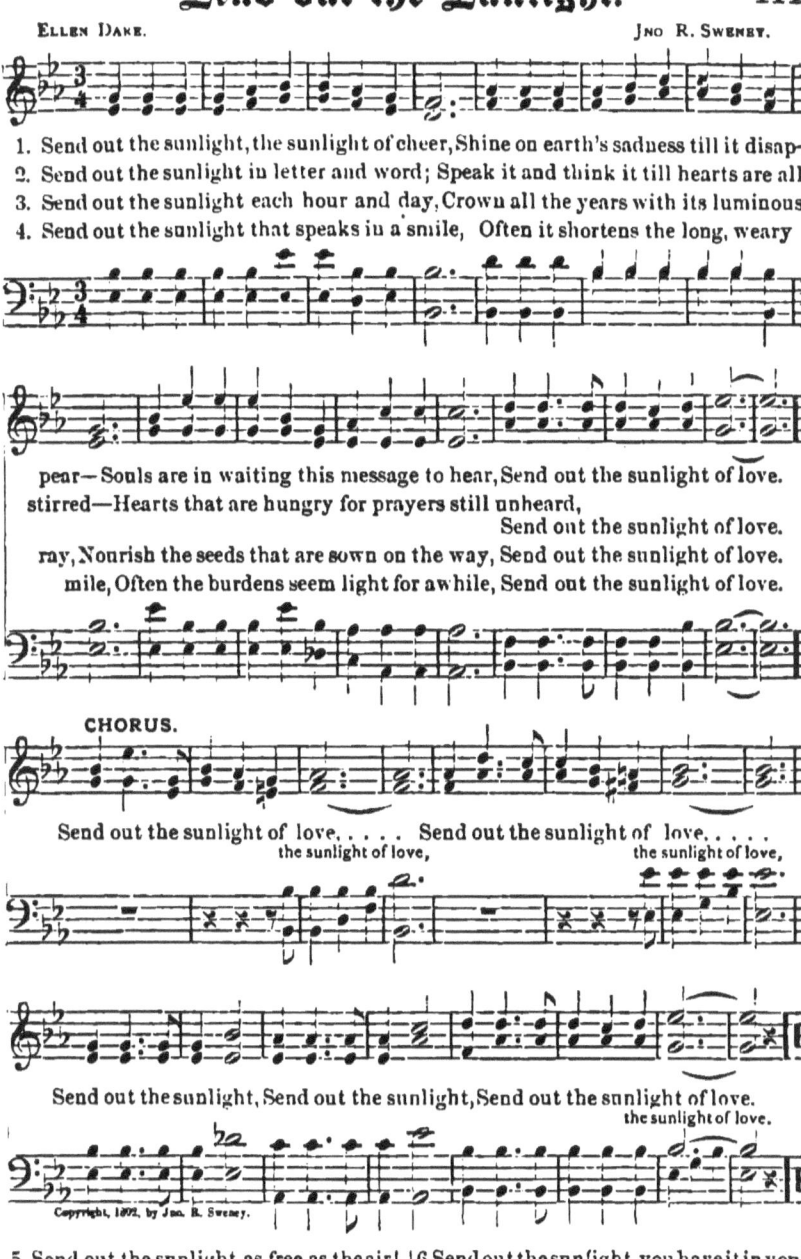

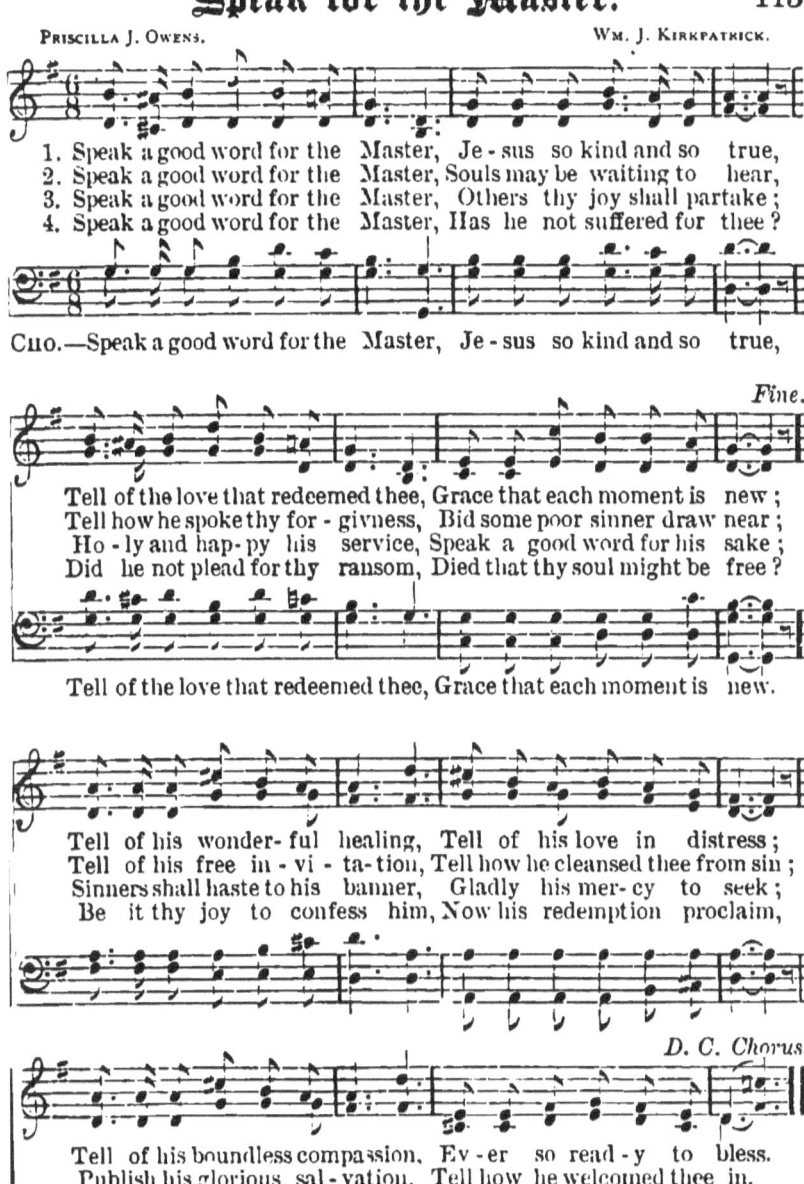

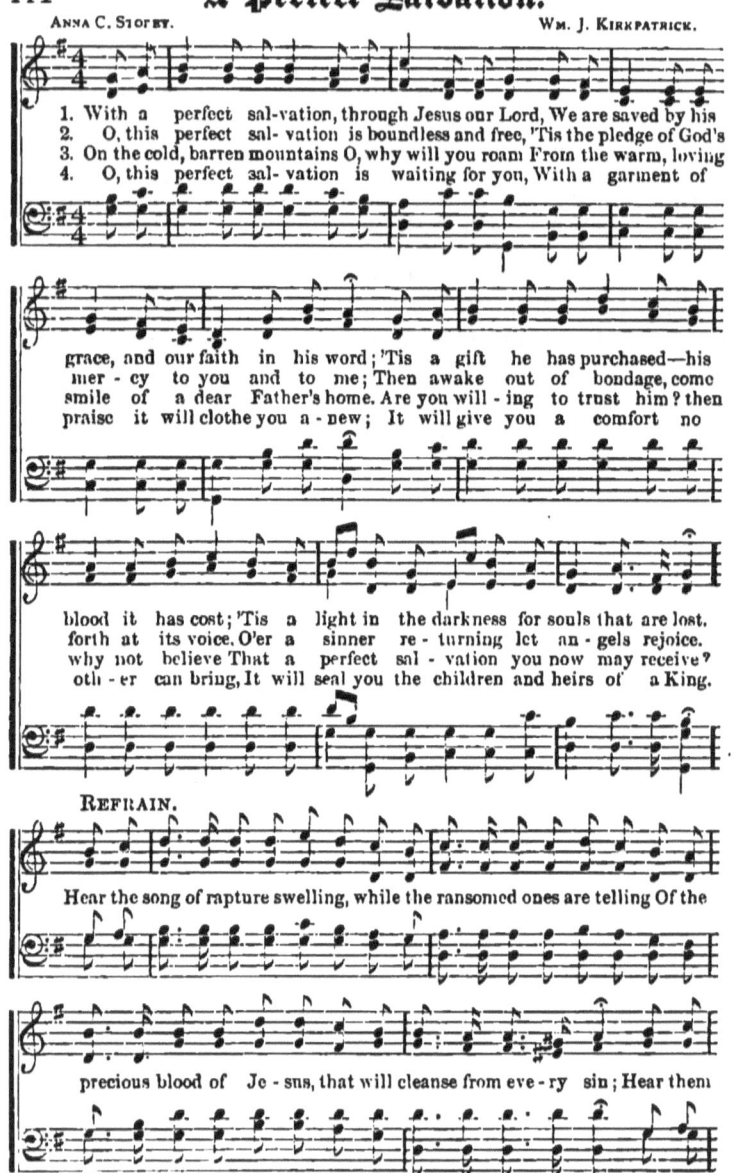

A Perfect Salvation.—CONCLUDED.

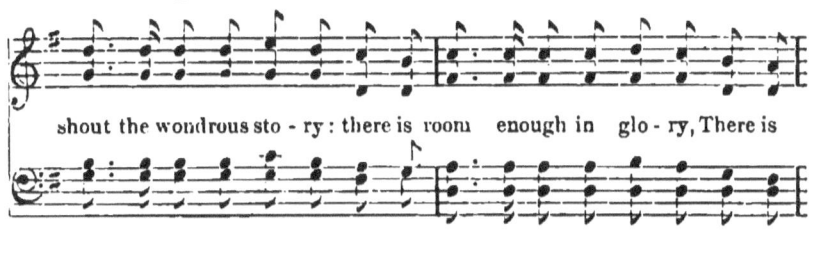

shout the wondrous sto-ry: there is room enough in glo-ry, There is room e-nough in glo-ry for the world to en-ter in.

Surrendered.

H. L. G.
Dr. H. L. GILMOUR.

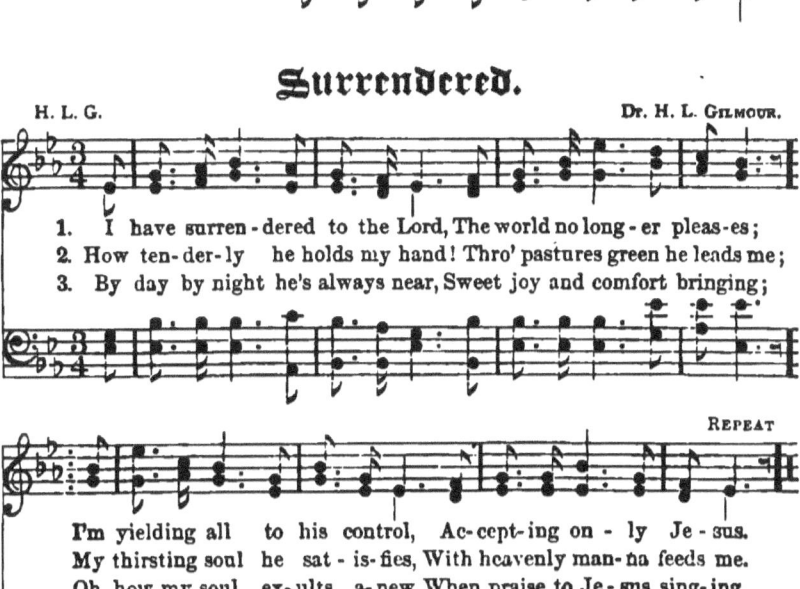

1. I have surren-dered to the Lord, The world no long-er pleas-es;
2. How ten-der-ly he holds my hand! Thro' pastures green he leads me;
3. By day by night he's always near, Sweet joy and comfort bringing;

I'm yielding all to his control, Ac-cept-ing on-ly Je-sus.
My thirsting soul he sat-is-fies, With heavenly man-na feeds me.
Oh, how my soul ex-ults a-new When praise to Je-sus sing-ing.

4 No noonday drought affects my soul,
  In Jesus I'm confiding;
Oh, constant, sweet companionship,
  With Christ in me abiding.

5 Oh, victory that's always sure!
  Oh, blest emancipation!
Oh, vanquished tempter of my soul!
  Oh, free and full salvation!

Copyright, 1885, by JOHN J. HOOD.

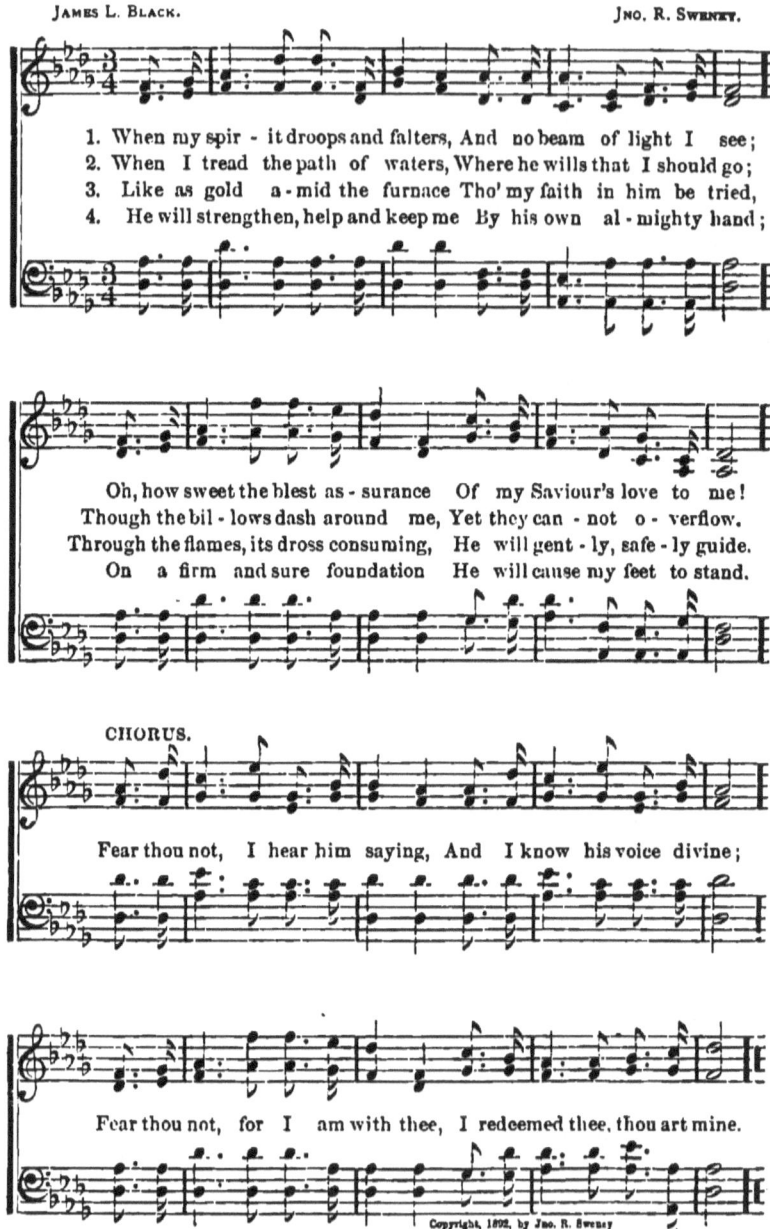

In the Master's Name. 117

E. A. Barnes. Wm. J. Kirkpatrick.

1. Are we sowing, with a ready hand, Gospel words that hold the precious seed?
2. Are we seeking to reclaim the lost, By his call so tender and so sweet?
3. Are we speaking for the good of all, Gospel words of his redeeming love?
4. Are we liv- ing in his service here, Serving well, our love and zeal to show?

Are we helping, with a loving heart, Where are seen so many in their need?
Are we praying that the world at large May be brought to worship at his feet?
Are we bearing to the heart of grief Precious balm of comfort from above?
Are we giving with a will- ing heart, To advance his kingdom here below?

CHORUS.

Are we do - ing this? Are we do - ing this? Working while we may?

In the Master's name, For the Master's sake, La- bor while 'tis day.

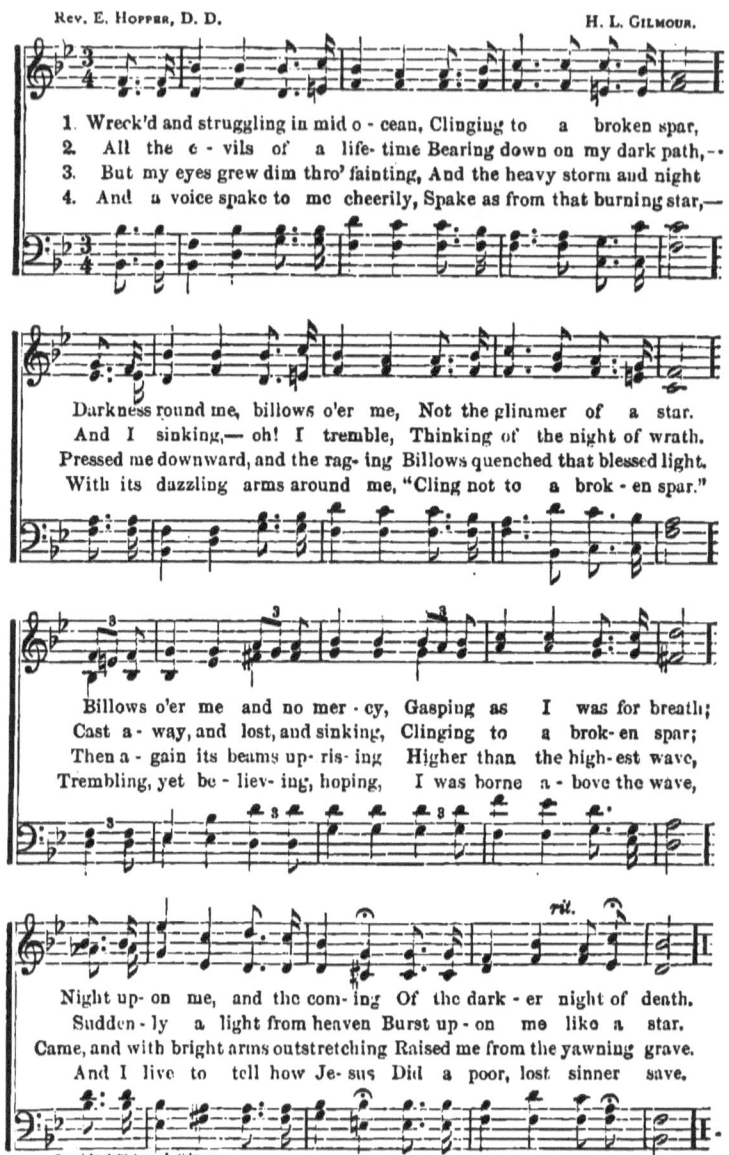

Hasten to the Fountain.

WILLIAM HENRY GARDNER.   JNO. R. SWENEY.

1. Sinner, fear not, Je- sus loves thee, And for thee he surely died;
2. Freely flows the blessed fountain, Whoso - ev - er will may go;
3. Oh, what joy wells up within thee When thy sins are washed away!
4. Turn, O sin - ner, from thy e - vil, Seek the gracious Lord to - day;

For thy sins and mine he suffered, On the cross was cru - ci - fied.
Plunge beneath the liv- ing wa- ters, And the "great salvation" know.
Joy and hope are ev - er with thee, Growing brighter ev - 'ry day.
Though thy sins be red as crim- son, He will wash them all a- way.

CHORUS.

Though thy sins be red as crimson, They shall be as white as snow;
Though thy sins   They shall be

Sin- ner, hast - en to the fountain, Where the healing waters flow.
Sinner, hasten

Soul Rest.

MARY A. WHITAKER. Cho. H. L. G. Matt. xi: 29. H. L. GILMOUR.

1. Saviour, we come to thee Weary and weak, Help for our burdened hearts Trusting we seek; Take thou our weariness In - to thy rest, Shelter our weakness, Lord, Safe in thy breast.
2. On - ly in thee we find Resting and peace, Stilled by thy voice divine Conflict will cease: Kindly and tender - ly Falleth thy word, Bidding us fearless come Close to thee, Lord.
3. Close to thee ev - ermore, Led by thy hand; Fed from thy bounteous heart, Strong we shall stand; Welcome our human lot, Stern tho' it be, Sweet will its labors prove, Done as for thee.
4. Thus may we rise beyond All this world's strife, Owning thy righteous will, Living thy life; Faithfully serving thee, True to thy love, Till we are called to rest With thee above.

CHORUS.

Eas - y thy yoke, so suit - ed to me, Burdens made light by com - ing to thee; Rest- ing in la - bor, and walk - ing in light, Hap - py in Je - sus, oh, bless - ed de - light.

Copyright, 1892, by H. L. Gilmour.

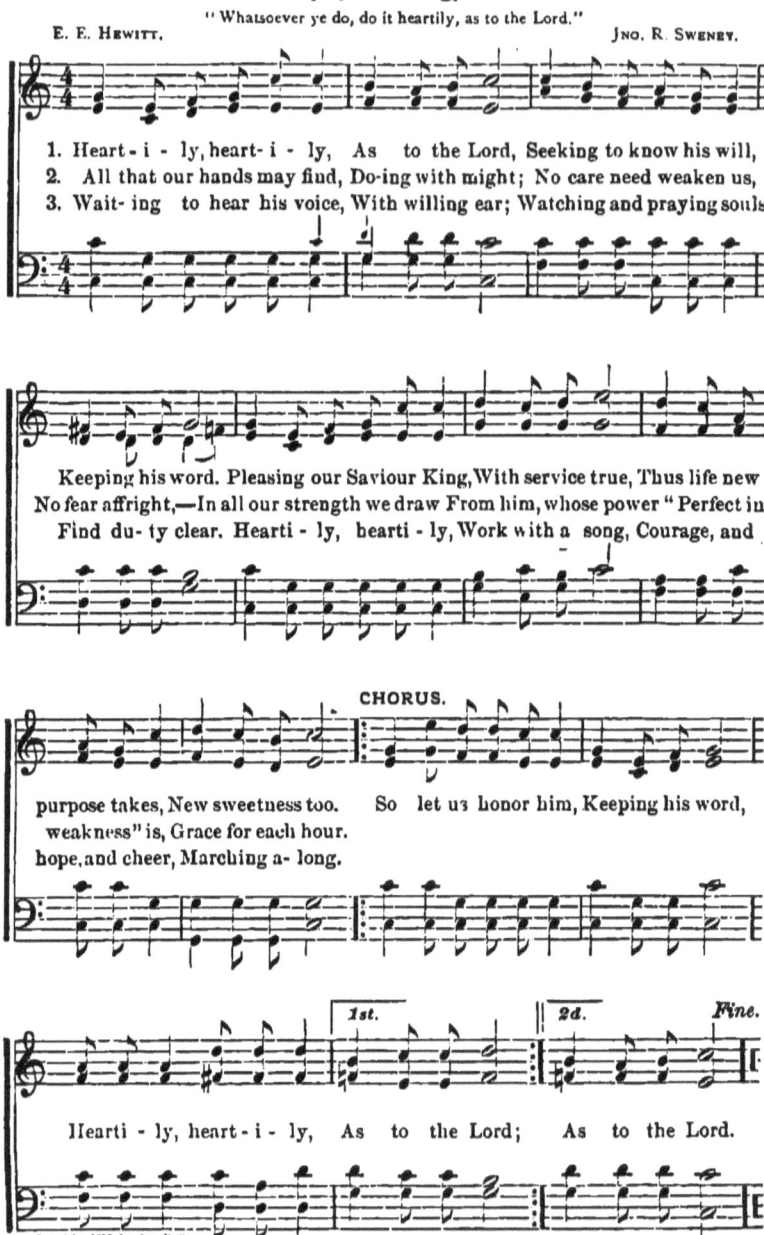

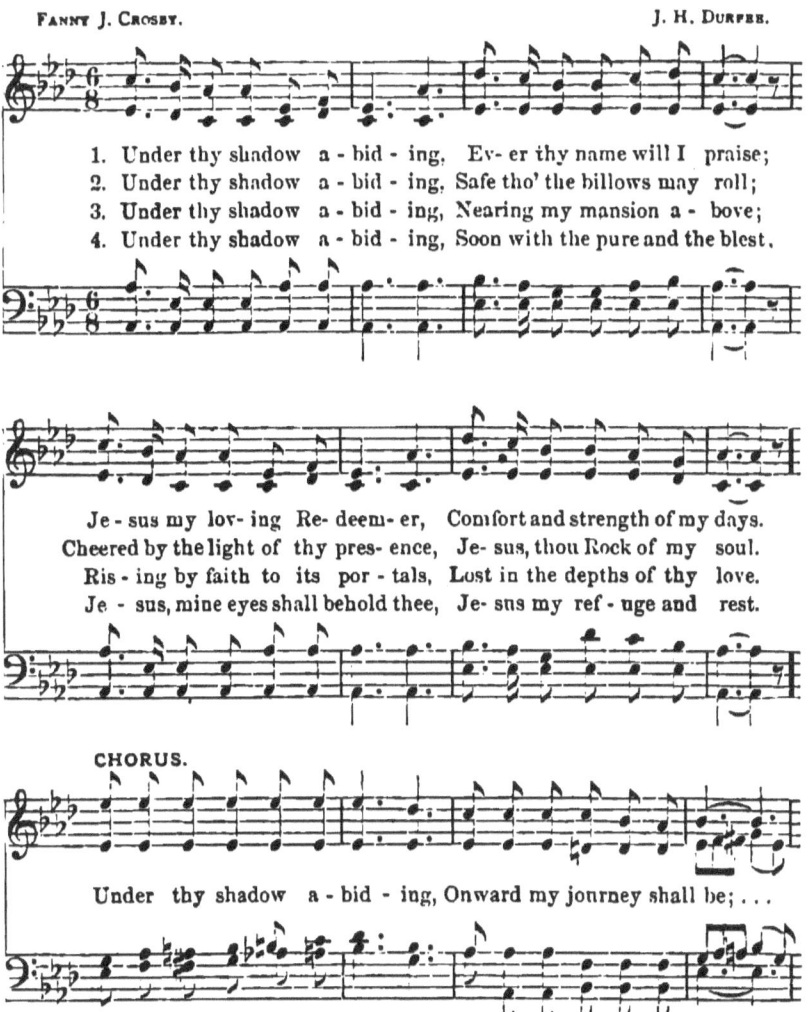

126. There's a Word for Me.

L. H. Edmunds.   Jno. R. Sweney.

1. There's a word for me in the blessed book, I can see it there ev'ry time I look; And a sweet-er word there can nev-er be Than my Saviour's call, "come, oh, come to me."
2. "Whoso-ev-er will," precious word to me, So I humbly came to the wa-ters free; While I drink with joy from sal-va-tion's tide, Ev-'ry need in Jesus will be supplied.
3. There's no earthly fount that can satis-fy, But a blessing flows in the des-ert dry, For there's mention made in the bless-ed book, Of a "way" made glad by the living "brook."
4. Let the wondrous word thro' the wide world ring, Oh, that all would drink of the heavenly spring! Oh, that all would come unto Christ and live, Take the mighty grace that he loves to give.

CHORUS.

Whosoever! whosoever! Sweeter word can nev-er be; Whosoever! whosoever Surely this was meant for me.

Copyright, 1892, by Jno. R. Sweney.

128. My Song of Joy.

JENNIE GARNETT.
JNO. R. SWENEY.

SOLO or DUET.

1. I am learn-ing a song that with joy I shall sing When the toils of my journey are done, When by grace I can say, I have finished my course, And the crown thro' the cross I have won.
2. I am learn-ing a song that with joy I shall sing When the sleep of a moment is o'er, And I wake with a shout at the por-tals of bliss, In the pres-ence of him I a-dore.
3. I am learn-ing a song that with joy I shall sing When the ransomed in glo-ry I meet, When the voice of my Saviour shall welcome me there, And I lay down my cross at his feet.
4. I am learn-ing a song that with joy I shall sing When my soul is un-fet-tered and free; I am learning a song that for-ev-er shall ring, And its ech-o re-ech-oed shall be.

Copyright, 1884, by Jno. R. Sweney.

My Song of Joy.—CONCLUDED.

1 With tearful eyes I look around;
Life seems a dark and | stormy | sea ;
Yet 'midst the gloom I hear a sound,
A heavenly | whisper, | Come to | me.

2 It tells me of a place of rest,
It tells me where my | soul may | flee ;
Oh, to the weary, faint, opprest,
How sweet the | bidding, | Come to | me!

3 When nature shudders, loth to part
From all I love, en- | joy and | see,

When a faint chill steals o'er my heart,
A sweet voice | utters, | Come to | me.

4 Come, for all else must fail and die,
Earth is no resting- | place for | thee ;
Heavenward direct thy weeping eye;
I am thy | portion ; | come to | me.

5 O voice of mercy, voice of love!
In conflict, grief and | ago- | ny,
Support me, cheer me from above,
And gently | whisper, | Come to | me.

Winning Songs—I

130. Anchor Me Home.

FANNY J. CROSBY. WM. J. KIRKPATRICK.

1. Graciously, tenderly, Jesus my Saviour Stands at the helm when the
2. Hopefully, prayerfully, trusting thy promise, What is the world or its
3. Tranquilly, peacefully, while I am going, Bright are the visions that
4. Stead-i-ly, earnestly, Je-sus my Saviour, Help me with vigor to

dark billows foam; O-ver life's o-cean my vessel di-recting,
changes to me? Thou art my Refuge, I ask for no oth-er,
burst on my sight; Nearer and nearer my soul is approaching
bend to the oar; Oh, what a prospect of rapture before me!

D.S.—O-ver life's o-cean my vessel di-recting,

Fine. CHORUS.

Lead to the har-bor, and an-chor me home. An-chor me home,
I have com-mit-ted my all un-to thee.
Riv-ers of pleas-ure in vales of de-light.
Soon and for-ev-er I'll rest on the shore.

Lead to the har-bor, and an-chor me home.

D.S.

anchor me home, Never again from thy presence to roam;

Copyright, 1.92, by Wm. J. Kirkpatrick.

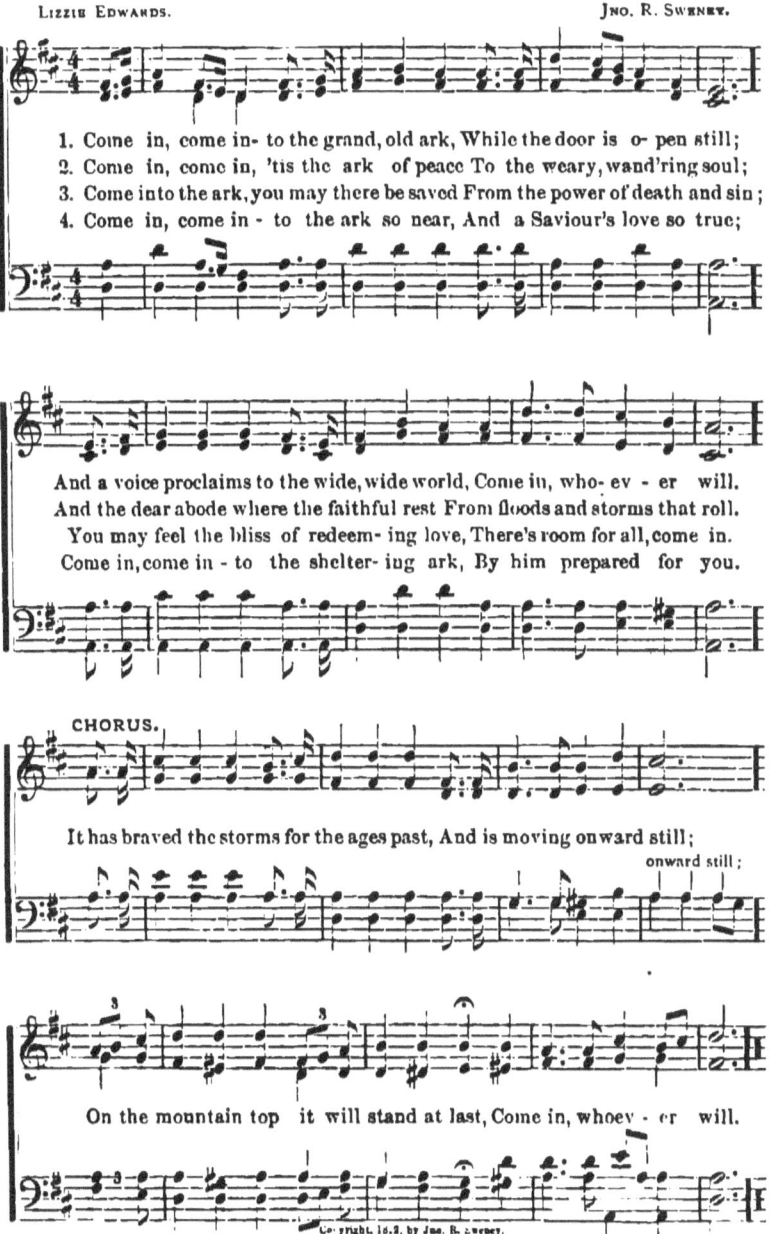

There's a Song, etc.—CONCLUDED. 133

on - ly a child, Bending low at my dear mother's knee, And I
mer - cy of God, And sorrow soon conquered my pride; As I
gladness of hope, As once up- on dark Gal- i - lee, Trampled
day of my life, And ris - ing to mountains of joy, Where com-

love it to-day; I shall love it alway, For bringing such blessings to me.
looked thro' my tears my Saviour appeared, And said that for me he had died.
down the rough waves, and cried out," it is I, Fear not, cast your care upon me."
munion with God is perfection of bliss, His work is my grandest employ.

CHORUS.

Oh, glory to God for the gift of his Son, Proclaiming salvation is free; . . . .
it is free;

And faith, simple faith brings it down to each one, Oh, glory, it brings it to me.

134. That Meeting to Come.

E. R. LATTA. WM. J. KIRKPATRICK.

Moderato con espress.

1. Are you getting read-y, brother, For that meeting to come? There is
2. Are you getting read-y, sinner, For that meeting to come? What ex-
3. All the ho-ly shall be ready, In that meeting to come! They shall
4. There shall many be re-jected, In that meeting to come! The un-

CHORUS.

need of prepar-ation, For that meeting to come! When the books of heav'n
cus-es can you of-fer, In that meeting to come! [are
car-ry palms of vict'ry, In that meeting to come!
god-ly and the sinful, In that meeting to come!

opened, In that meeting to come, Shall you hear the Saviour's welcome,

In that meeting to come? In that meeting to come, In that meeting to come,

ritard. ad lib.

Shall you hear the Saviour's welcome, In that meeting to come?

Copyright, 1892, by Wm. J. Kirkpatrick.

5 What rejoicing for the righteous,
  In that meeting to come!
"Come, ye blessed!" there shall greet
  In that meeting to come! [them,

6 What remorse shall seize the wicked,
  In that meeting to come!
When they hear their awful sentence,
  In that meeting to come!

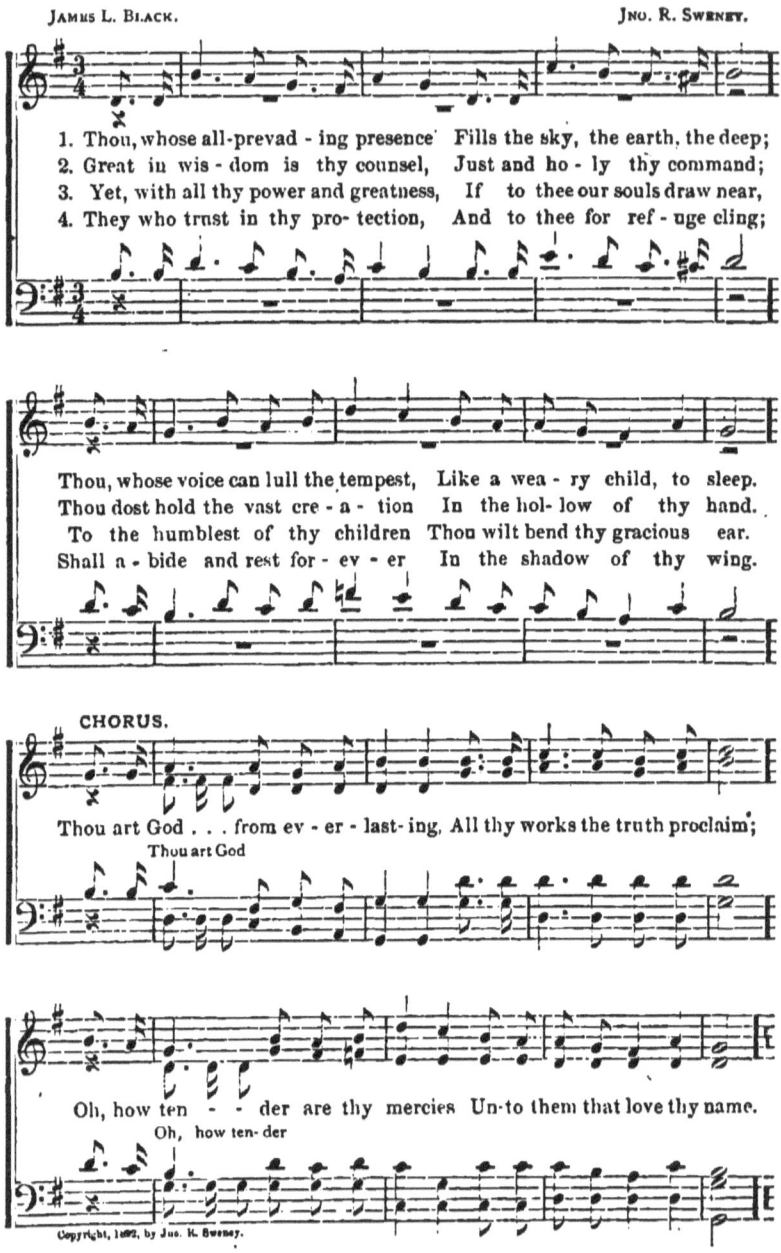

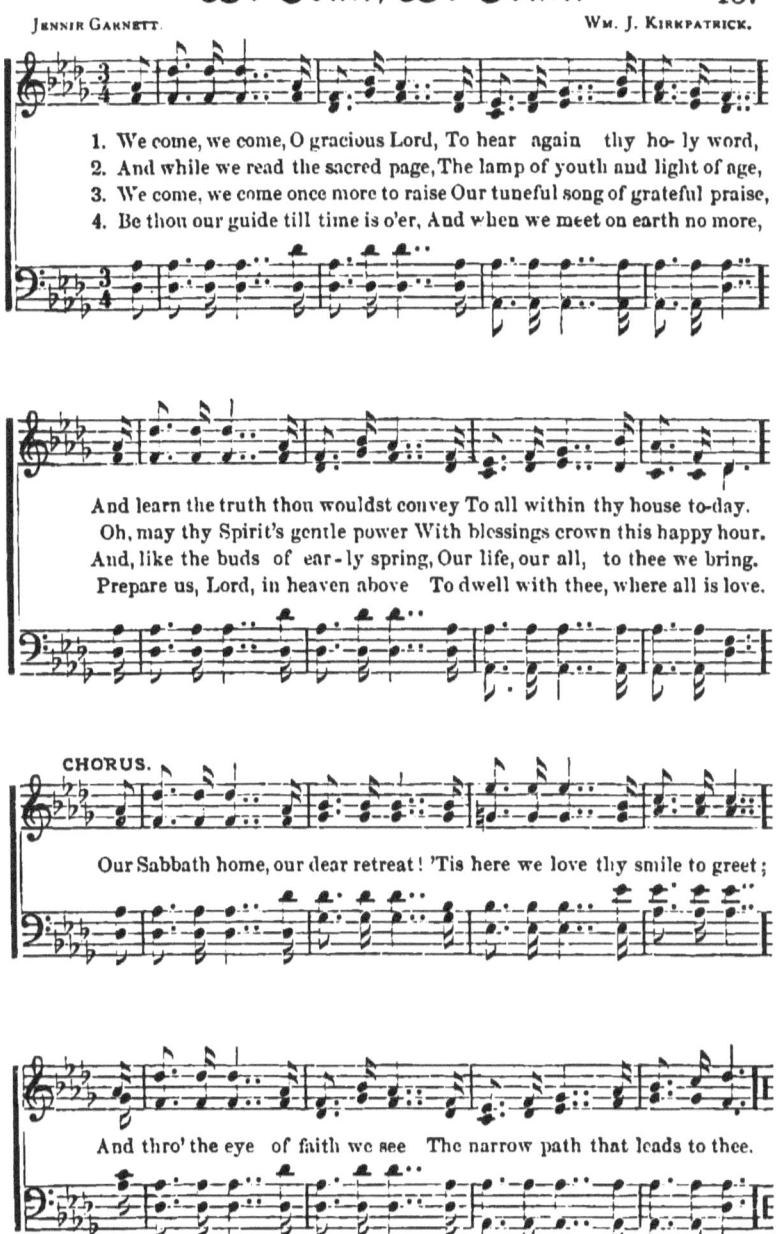

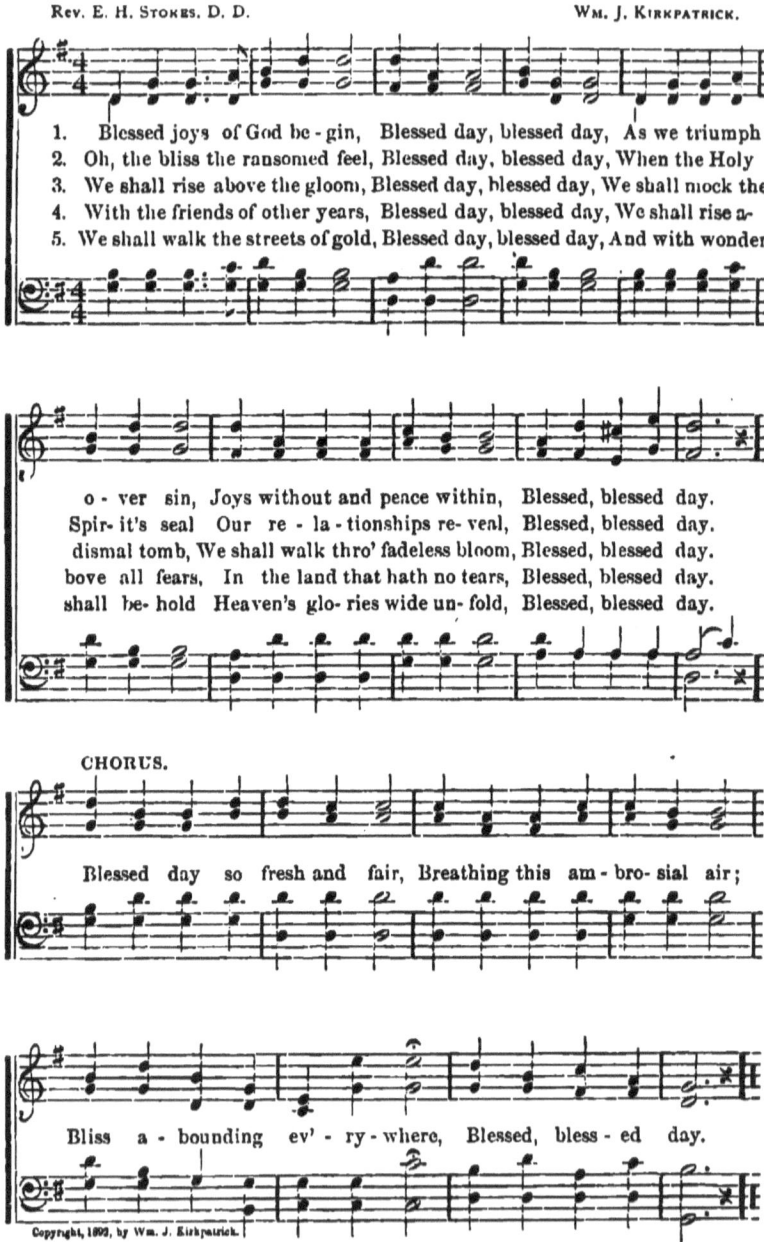

Perfect in Thee. 139

WM. J. ORTLIP. JNO. R. SWENEY.

1. I long to be perfect, my Saviour, in thee, To feel thou art ev-er a-biding in me; I long in the fulness of rapture to rise.
2. I long to be nearer, still near-er thy throne, O cleanse me each moment and keep me thine own; I long to be like thee in spirit and mind,
3. I long to be humble, conformed to thy will, To walk in thy shadow and follow thee still; My cross-es and tri-als with patience to bear,
4. And when to thy mansion thou call-est a-way, When lost in the splendor of in-fi-nite day; I wake to behold thee, my Saviour, above,

And bask in thy glory that breaks from the skies.
Obeying thy counsel, in all things resigned.
And trust in thy mercy for answer to prayer.
I'll praise thee forever and sing of thy love.

CHORUS.

Perfect in thee, . . perfect in thee, . . .
perfect in thee,

I long to be perfect, my Saviour, in thee; Perfect in thee, . . perfect in thee, . . I long to perfect, my Saviour, in thee.
perfect in thee,

Copyright, 1892, by Jno R. Sweney.

Lord, I'm Coming Home.

W. J. K.
With great feeling.
Wm. J. Kirkpatrick.

1. I've wandered far a-way from God, Now I'm coming home;
2. I've wast-ed ma-ny pre-cious years, Now I'm coming home;
3. I'm tired of sin and stray-ing, Lord, Now I'm coming home;
4. My soul is sick, my heart is sore, Now I'm coming home;

The paths of sin too long I've trod, Lord, I'm coming home.
I now re-pent with bit-ter tears, Lord, I'm coming home.
I'll trust thy love, be-lieve thy word, Lord, I'm coming home.
My strength renew, my hope re-store, Lord, I'm coming home.

D.S.—O-pen wide thine arms of love, Lord, I'm coming home.

CHORUS.

Coming home, coming home, Nev-er more to roam;

Copyright, 1892, by Wm. J. Kirkpatrick.

5 My only hope, my only plea,
Now I'm coming home.
That Jesus died, and died for me,
Lord, I'm coming home.

6 I need his cleansing blood I know,
Now I'm coming home;
Oh, wash me whiter than the snow,
Lord, I'm coming home.

The Unclouded Day.

(May be used as a Solo.)

Words and Melody by Rev. J. K. Alwood.   Harmony by J. F. Kinsey.

1. O they tell me of a home far beyond the skies, O they tell me of a home far away; O they tell me of a home where no storm-clouds rise, O they tell me of an unclouded day; O the land of cloudless day, O the land of an un-cloud-ed sky; O they tell me of a
2. O they tell me of a home where my friends have gone, O they tell me of that land far away; Where the tree of life in e-ter-nal bloom, Sheds its fragrance thro' the unclouded day; O the land of cloudless day, O the land of an un-cloud-ed sky; O they tell me of my
3. O they tell me of the King in his beauty there, And they tell that mine eyes shall behold Where he sits on the throne that is whiter than snow, In the cit-y that is made of gold; O that land mine eyes shall see, O that land of an un-cloud-ed sky; O they tell me of the
4. O they tell me that he smiles on his children there, And his smile drives their sorrows all a-way; And they tell me that no tears ev-er come a-gain, In that lovely land of unclouded day; O that land of love-ly smiles, O the smiles of his love-beaming eye; O the King in his

By per. of The Echo Music Co.

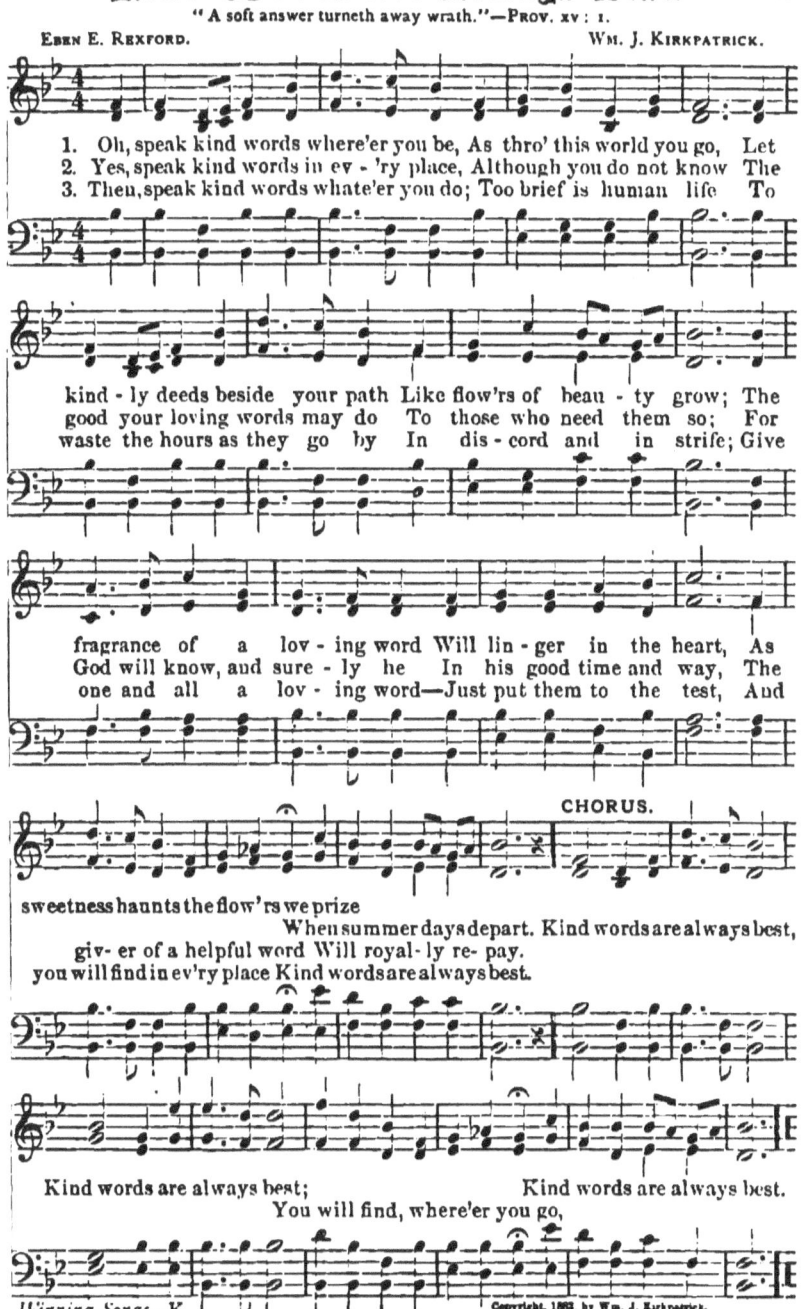

It will Never Grow Old.

"And the city had no need of the sun: for the glory of God did lighten it."—Rev. xxi: 23.

Rev. W. W. Baily. I. N. McHose. By per.

1. O have you not heard of that country a-bove, The name of its King, and his in-fi-nite love? His children are deathless and hap-py, I'm told; Oh, will it a-bide, will it never grow old?
2. That wonder-ful land has a cit-y of life, Ne'er darken'd with anguish, nor dy-ing, nor strife; Its tem-ples and streets all are flashing with gold, Oh, can it be true, it will never grow old?
3. A mansion of wonder-ful beauty is there, And Je-sus that mansion has gone to pre-pare; Its bright jas-per walls how I long to be-hold, And join in the song that will never grow old.
4. They tell me its friendships and love are so pure, Its joys never die, and its treasures are sure; And loved ones, depart-ed, so si-lent and cold, Will greet us a-gain where we'll never grow old.

D.S.—joy that's untold, To think of that land that will never grow old.

CHORUS.

'Twill always be new, it will nev-er de-cay; No night ev-er comes, it will al-ways be day; It glad-dens my heart with a

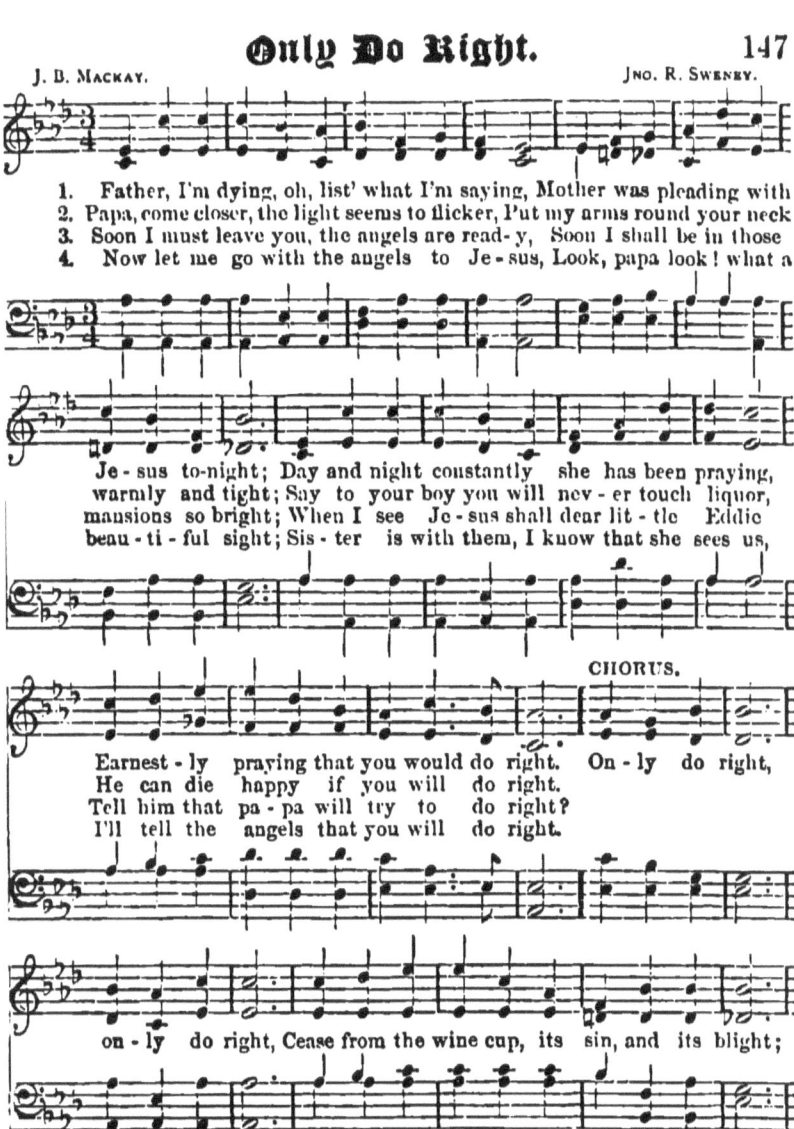

Going Home to Be, etc.—CONCLUDED. 149

home, Going home to be with Jesus, to be blest forevermore.
going home,

Give Glory to Jesus.

PRISCILLA J. OWENS.   WM. J. KIRKPATRICK.

1. Give glory to Je- sus, who lives and reigns, Give glory to Je - sus, who
2. Give glory to Je- sus, he walks the waves, Give glory to Je - sus, he
3. Give glory to Je- sus, he wakes the tomb, Give glory to Je - sus, he

breaks our chains; He sets the captive exile free, His voice shall sound the jubilee.
hears and saves; His whisper stills the raging tide, Before his feet the floods divide.
breaks death's gloom; He turns the shadow of the night
                                    To dawning fair, and glorious light.

CHORUS.

Give glory to Jesus, give glory to Jesus, Give glory to Je- sus o'er and o'er;

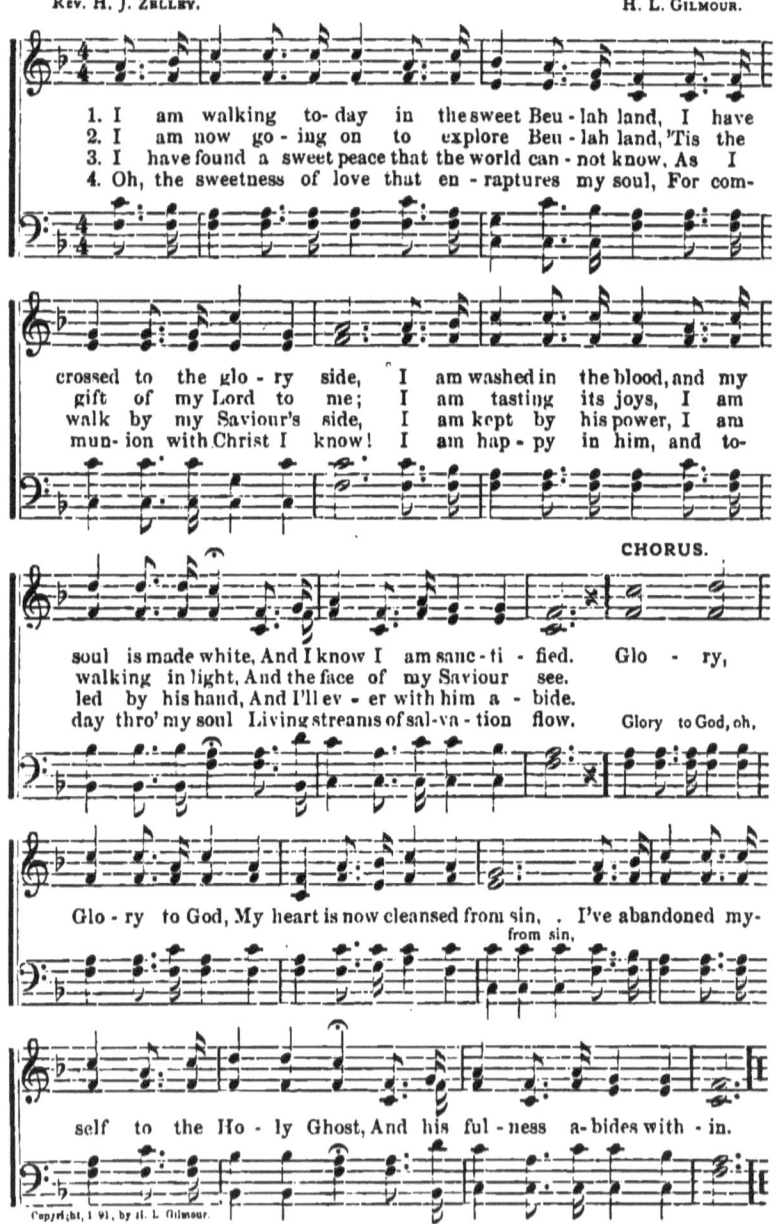

152. Marching on to Canaan.

"They shall march with an army."—Jer. xlvi: 22.

Rev. M. Lowrie Hofford. — W. A. Ogden, By per.

1. We are marching on to Canaan, And Jehovah is our guide;
   We are marching thro' the desert, He is ever at our side;
2. We are marching thro' the desert, And the manna all around
   With the dew of night is falling, And is cov'ring all the ground;
3. We are marching thro' the desert To the promised land divine,
   To the land of milk and honey, To the land of corn and wine;

DUET.

In the darkness or the danger   We can never go astray,
From the smitten rock the waters   In their sparkling fulness flow,
We are marching thro' the desert,   We approach the shining shore.

With Jehovah for our leader   And our guide upon the way.
Thus delighting and refreshing   Us the weary journey through.
From our home beyond the Jordan   We shall wander never more.

FULL CHORUS.

On, steadily on!   Steadily marching to the happy land of
Marching on, marching on,   we're

Copyright, 1885, by W. A. Ogden.

Marching on to Canaan.—CONCLUDED. 153

Ca - naan; On, steadi-ly on! Veri-ly guid-ed by Je-
marching on, Marching on, marching on, Stedily marching to the
hovah's hand are we, (guided are we). hap - py land we go. (marching home).

Jesus, my Saviour.

Rev. J. B. FRENCH.   WM. J. KIRKPATRICK.

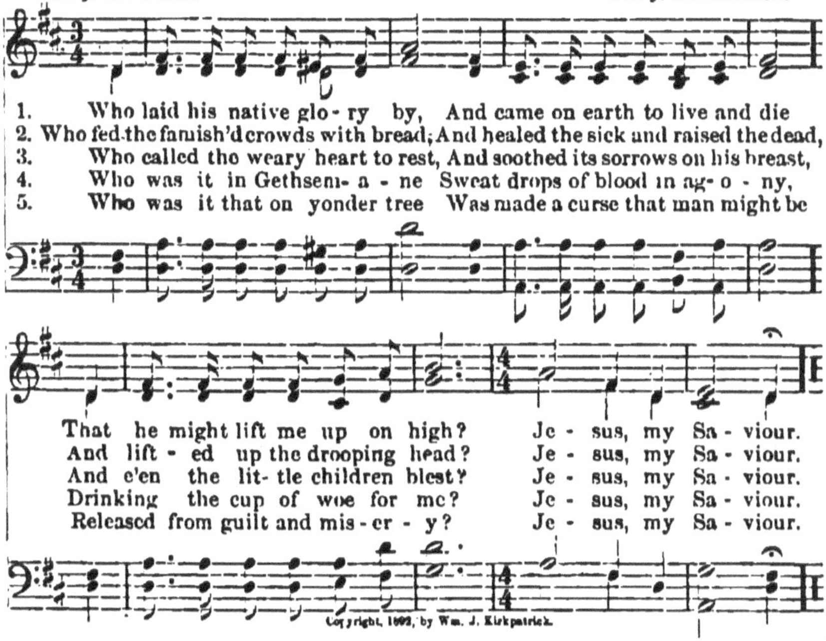

1. Who laid his native glo - ry by, And came on earth to live and die
2. Who fed the famish'd crowds with bread; And healed the sick and raised the dead,
3. Who called the weary heart to rest, And soothed its sorrows on his breast,
4. Who was it in Gethsem- a - ne Sweat drops of blood in ag- o - ny,
5. Who was it that on yonder tree Was made a curse that man might be

That he might lift me up on high? Je - sus, my Sa - viour.
And lift - ed up the drooping head? Je - sus, my Sa - viour.
And e'en the lit- tle children blest? Je - sus, my Sa - viour.
Drinking the cup of woe for me? Je - sus, my Sa - viour.
Released from guilt and mis - er - y? Je - sus, my Sa - viour.

Copyright, 1892, by Wm. J. Kirkpatrick.

6 O Christ, and could it ever be
That once I felt no love for thee,
Thou loving Lord of Calvary,—
Jesus, my Saviour.

7 But now mine eyes awake to see
What pains and griefs thou'st borne for
My heart, my life I give to thee,— [me,
Jesus, my Saviour.

Mercy is Boundless and Free. 157

HENRIETTA E. BLAIR. W. J. KIRKPATRICK.

1. Thanks be to Jesus, his mercy is free, Mercy is free, mercy is free;
2. Why on the mountains of sin wilt thou roam? Mercy is free, mercy is free;
3. Think of his goodness, his patience, and love, Mercy is free, mercy is free;
4. Yes, there is pardon for all who believe, Mercy is free, mercy is free;

REF.—Jesus the Saviour is looking for thee, looking for thee, looking for thee;

Sin-ner, that mercy is flowing for thee, Mercy is boundless and free.
Gently the Spirit is calling,"Come home." Mercy is boundless and free.
Pleading thy cause with his Father above, Mercy is boundless and free.
Come and this moment a blessing receive, Mercy is boundless and free

Loving-ly, tender-ly calling for thee, Calling and looking for thee.

If thou art willing on him to believe, Mercy is free, mercy is free;
Thou art in darkness, O, come to the light, Mercy is free, mercy is free;
Come and repenting, O, give him thy heart, Mercy is free, mercy is free;
Jesus is waiting, O, hear him proclaim, Mercy is free, mercy is free;

D.C. Refrain.

Life ev-er-lasting thy soul may receive, Mercy is boundless and free.
Je-sus is waiting, he'll save you to-night, Mercy is boundless and free.
Grieve him no longer, but come as thou art, Mercy is boundless and free.
Cling to his mercy, believe on his name, Mercy is boundless and free.

Copyright, 1892, by W. J. Kirkpatrick.

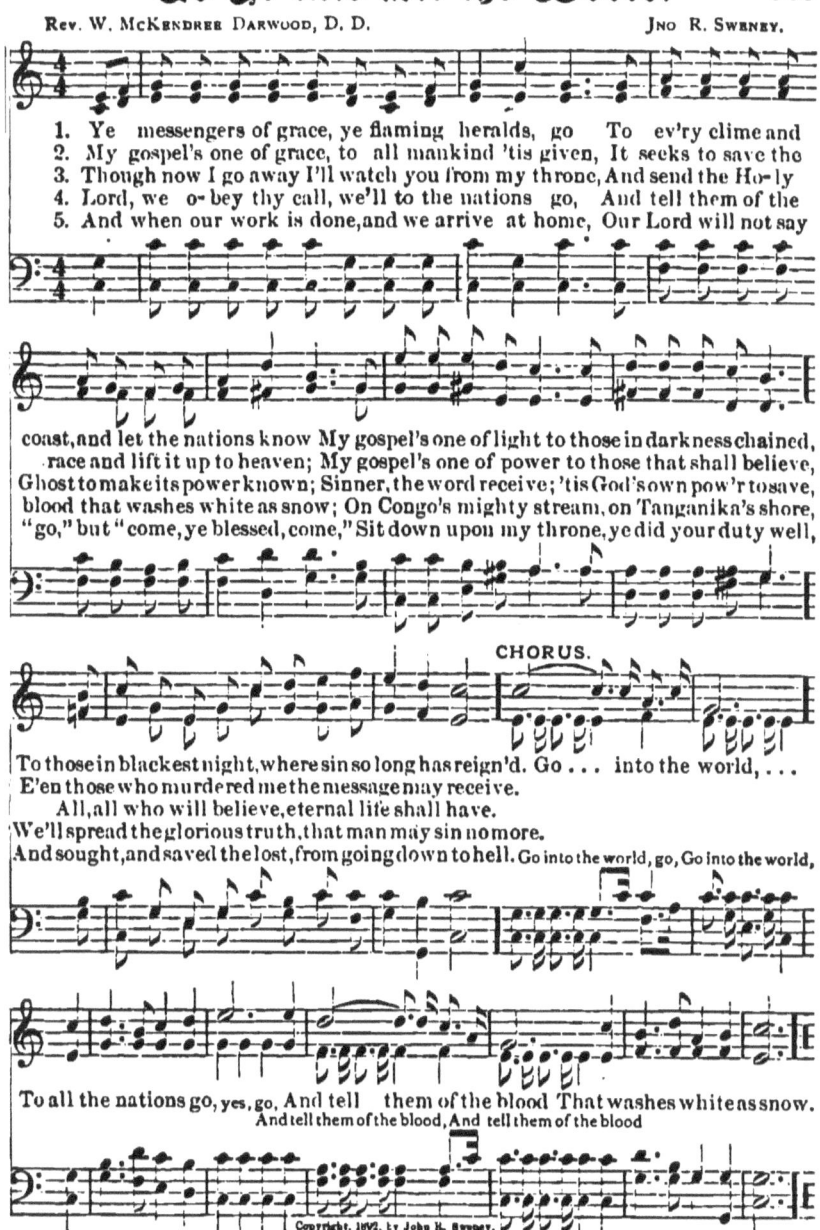

160. "This I Did for Thee."

H. Bonar. W. H. Doane.

Slow.

1. I gave my life for thee, My precious blood I shed, That thou might'st ransom'd be,
2. I spent long years for thee In weariness and woe, That one e-ter-ni-ty
3. My Father's house of light, My rainbow-circled throne, I left for earthly night,
4. I suffered much for thee,—More than my tongue can tell, Of bitterest agony;

And quickened from the dead; I gave my life for thee; What hast thou done for me?
Of joy thou mightest know; I spent long years for thee; Hast thou spent one for me?
For wand'rings sad and lone; I left it all all for thee; Hast thou left aught for me?
To rescue thee from hell; I suffered much for thee; What dost thou bear for me?

CHORUS.

This I did for thee,   What hast thou done for me?
This I did for thee, What hast thou done for me? Yes,

This I did for thee,   What hast thou done for me?
this I did for thee,

5 And I have brought to thee,
  Down from my house above,
  Salvation full and free.
  My pardon and my love;
  Great gifts I brought to thee;
  What hast thou brought to me?

6 Oh, let thy life be given,
  Thy years for me be spent,
  World fetters all be riven,
  And joy with suffering blent;
  Give thou thyself to me,
  And I will welcome thee!

Used by permission of with W. H. Doane, owner of Copyright.

The Sinner and the Song.—CONCLUDED. 163

SOLO.

O, tempter, de-part, I have served thee too long, I fly to the Saviour, he dwells in the song; O Lord, can it be that a sinner like me May find a sweet refuge by coming to thee?

QUARTET. *pp*

Oth-er refuge have I none; Hangs my helpless soul on thee.

SOLO.   **QUARTET.** *pp*

I come, Lord, I come, thou'lt forgive the dark past, And O, receive my soul at last.

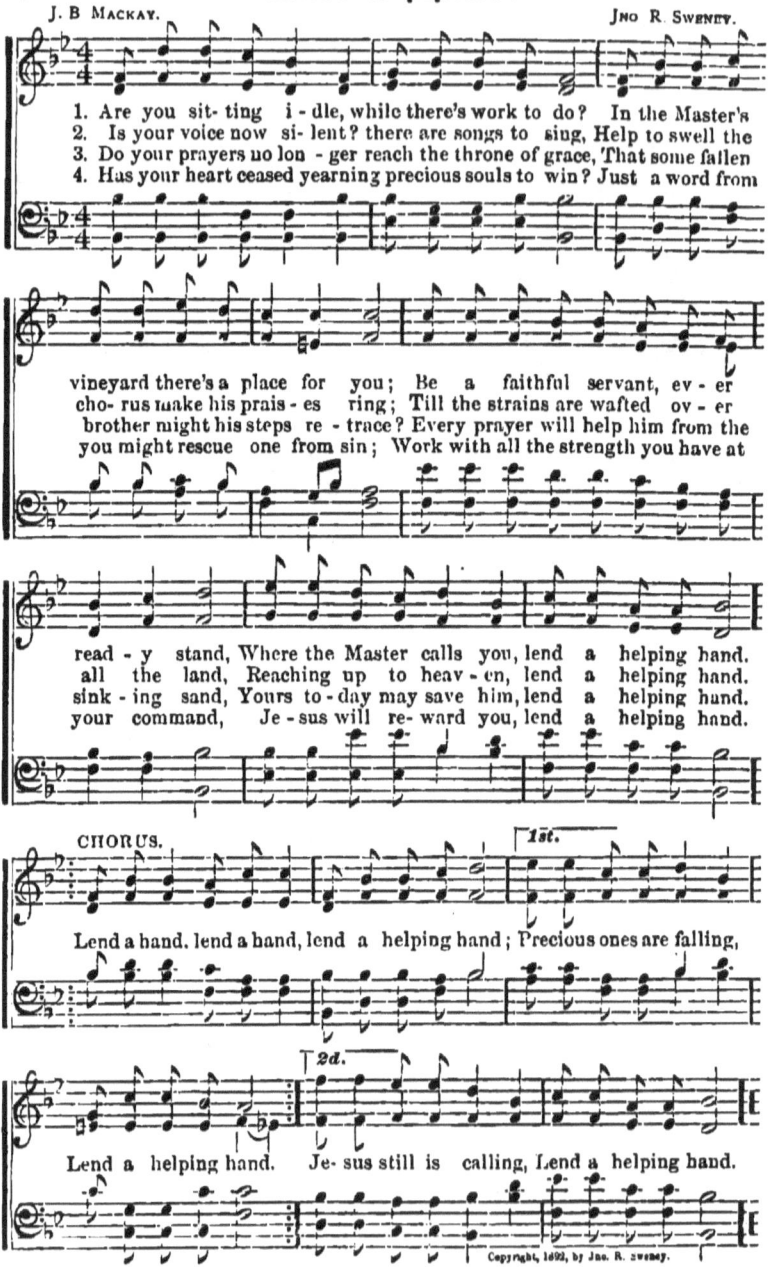

He is Just the Same, etc.—CONCLUDED. 167

CHORUS.

He's just the same to-day, Yes, just the same to-day, I'm glad to tell you, sinner, He is just the same to-day.

My Saviour.

DORA GREENWELL. WM. J. KIRKPATRICK.

1. I am not skill'd to understand What God hath will'd, what God hath plann'd;
2. I take God at his word and deed: "Christ died to save me," this I read,
3. And was there then no other way For God to take? I cannot say;
4. That he should leave his place on high, And come for sinful man to die,

I on-ly know at his right hand Stands one who is my Saviour.
And in my heart I find a need Of him to be my Saviour.
I on-ly bless him, day by day, Who saved me thro' my Saviour.
You count it strange?—so do not I, Since I have known my Saviour.

Copyright, 1885, by Wm. J. Kirkpatrick.

5 And, oh, that he fulfilled may see
The travail of his soul in me,
And with his work contented be,
  As I with my dear Saviour.

6 Yea, living, dying, let me bring
My strength, my solace from this spring,
That he who lives to be my King,
  Once died to be my Saviour.

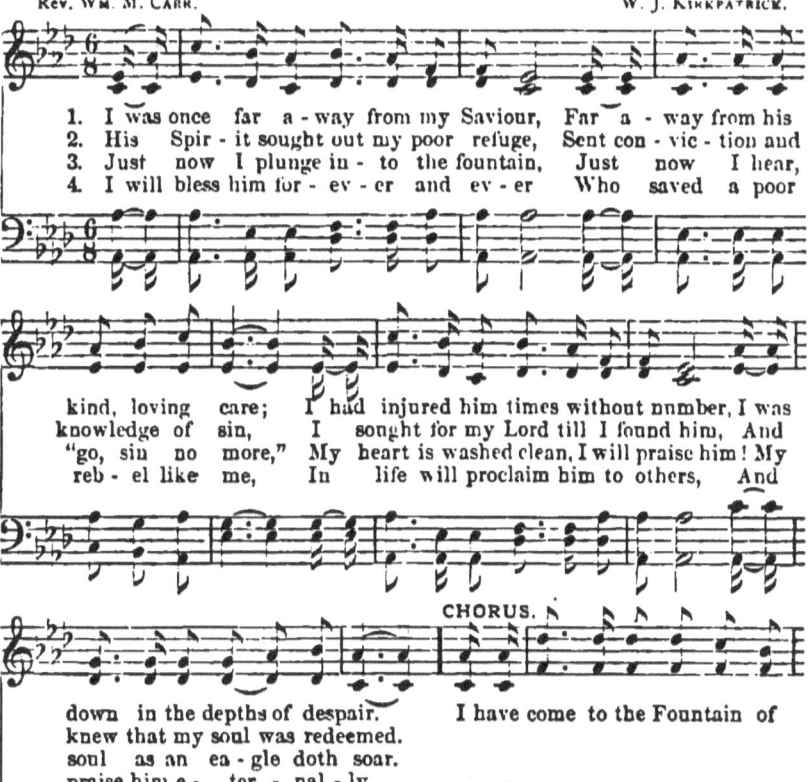

170. Stepping in the Light.

L. H. Edmunds.   W. J. Kirkpatrick.

1. Trying to walk in the steps of the Saviour, Trying to follow our
2. Pressing more closely to him who is leading, When we are tempted to
3. Walking in footsteps of gen-tle forbearance, Footsteps of faithfulness,
4. Trying to walk in the steps of the Saviour, Upward, still upward we'll

Saviour and King; Shaping our lives by his blessed ex-am-ple,
turn from the way; Trusting the arm that is strong to defend us,
mer-cy, and love, Looking to him for the grace free-ly promised,
fol-low our Guide, When we shall see him, "the King in his beauty."

CHORUS.

Happy, how happy, the songs that we bring, How beautiful to walk in the
Happy, how happy, our praises each day.
Happy, how happy, our journey above.
Happy, how happy, our place at his side.

steps of the Saviour, Stepping in the light, Stepping in the light; How

beautiful to walk in the steps of the Saviour, Led in paths of light.

Copyright, 1890, by Wm. J. Kirkpatrick.

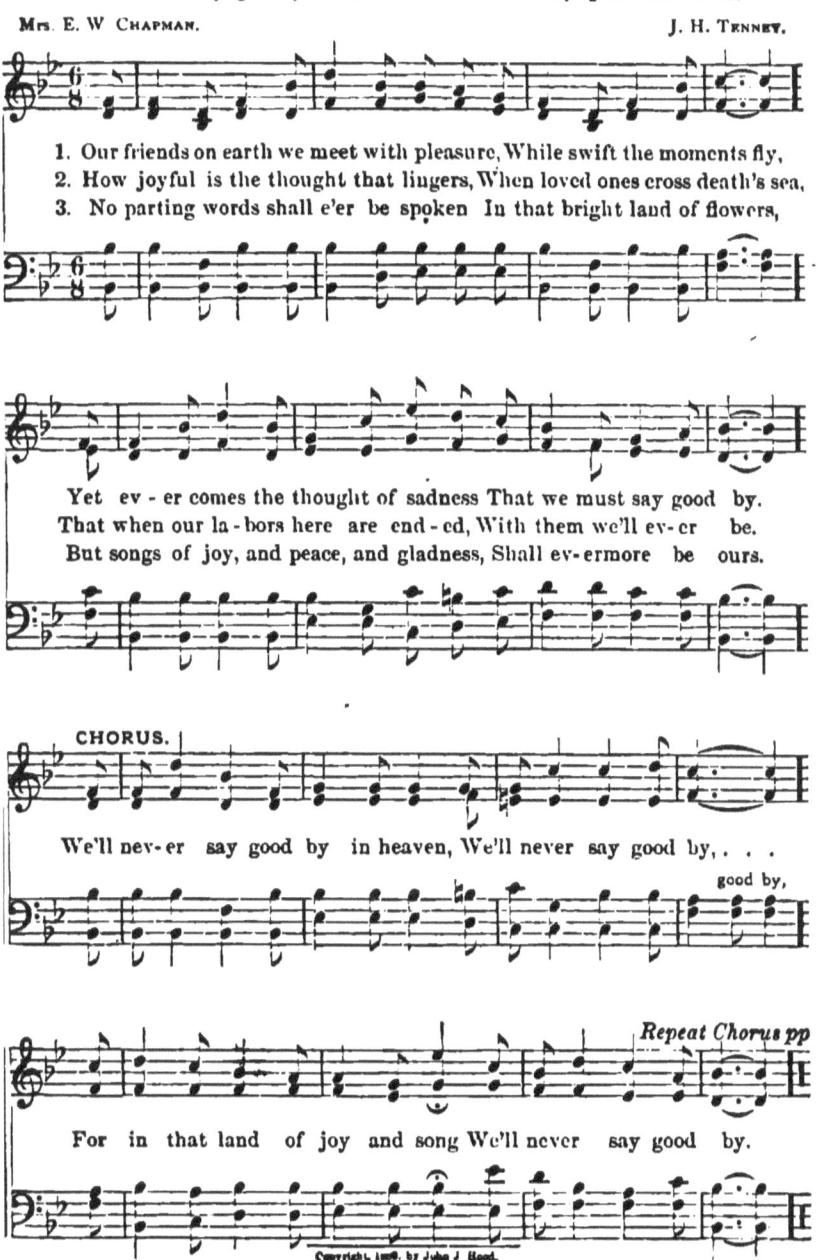

We'll Never Say Good By.

"We shall never say 'good by' in heaven."—The words of a dying Christian woman.

Mrs. E. W Chapman.   J. H. Tenney.

1. Our friends on earth we meet with pleasure, While swift the moments fly,
2. How joyful is the thought that lingers, When loved ones cross death's sea,
3. No parting words shall e'er be spoken In that bright land of flowers,

Yet ev-er comes the thought of sadness That we must say good by.
That when our la-bors here are end-ed, With them we'll ev-er be.
But songs of joy, and peace, and gladness, Shall ev-ermore be ours.

CHORUS.

We'll nev-er say good by in heaven, We'll never say good by, . . . good by,

Repeat Chorus pp

For in that land of joy and song We'll never say good by.

Copyright, 1880, by John J. Hood.

172. Ashamed of Jesus.

Grigg.
Jno. R. Sweney.

1. Je-sus, and shall . . . . it ev-er be, ... A mortal man . . . ashamed of thee? . . . Ashamed of thee, . . . whom angels praise, . . . Whose glories shine . . . thro' endless days.
2. Ashamed of Je - - - sus! sooner far . . . . Let evening blush . . . to own a star; . . He sheds the beams . . . of light divine, ... O'er this benight - - - - ed soul of mine.
3. Ashamed of Je - - - sus! just as soon . . . . Let midnight be . . . . ashamed of noon; . . 'Tis midnight with . . . my soul till he, ... Bright Morning Star, . . . bids darkness flee.
4. Ashamed of Je - - - sus! that dear Friend . . . On whom my hopes . . . of heav'n depend! . . No; when I blush, . . . be this my shame, . . . That I no more . . . . . revere his name.

CHORUS.

Ashamed of Jesus! never, No, nev-er, no, nev-er; Ashamed of Jesus! never, My best, my dearest Friend.

Copyright, 1892, by Jno. R. Sweney.

5 Ashamed of Jesus! yes, I may,
When I've no guilt to wash away;
No tear to wipe, no good to crave,
No fears to quell, no soul to save.

6 Till then—nor is my boasting vain—
Till then I boast a Saviour slain;
And oh, may this my glory be,
That Christ is not ashamed of me!

Jesus Comes.

Mrs. Phœbe Palmer.   Wm. J. Kirkpatrick.

1. Watch, ye saints, with eyelids waking, Lo, the pow'rs of heav'n are shaking,
Keep your lamps all trimm'd and burning, Ready for your Lord's return-ing.

2. Lo! the promise of your Saviour, Pardoned sin and purchased favor,
Blood-wash'd robes and crowns of glory; Haste to tell redemption's sto-ry.

3. Kingdoms at their base are crumbling, Hark, his chariot wheels are rumbling,
Tell, oh, tell of grace abounding, Whilst the seventh trump is sounding.

4. Nations wane, tho' proud and stately, Christ his kingdom hasteneth greatly,
Earth her lat-est pangs is summing, Shout, ye saints, your Lord is coming.

REFRAIN.
Lo! he comes, lo! Je-sus comes; Lo! he comes, he comes all glorious!
Je-sus comes to reign vic-torious, Lo! he comes, yes, Je-sus comes.

5. Lamb of God!—thou meek and lowly,
Judah's Lion!—high and holy,
Lo! thy bride comes forth to meet thee,
All in blood-washed robes to greet thee.

6. Sinners, come, while Christ is plead-ing;
Now for you he's in-terceding;
Haste, ere grace and time diminished
Shall proclaim the mystery finished.

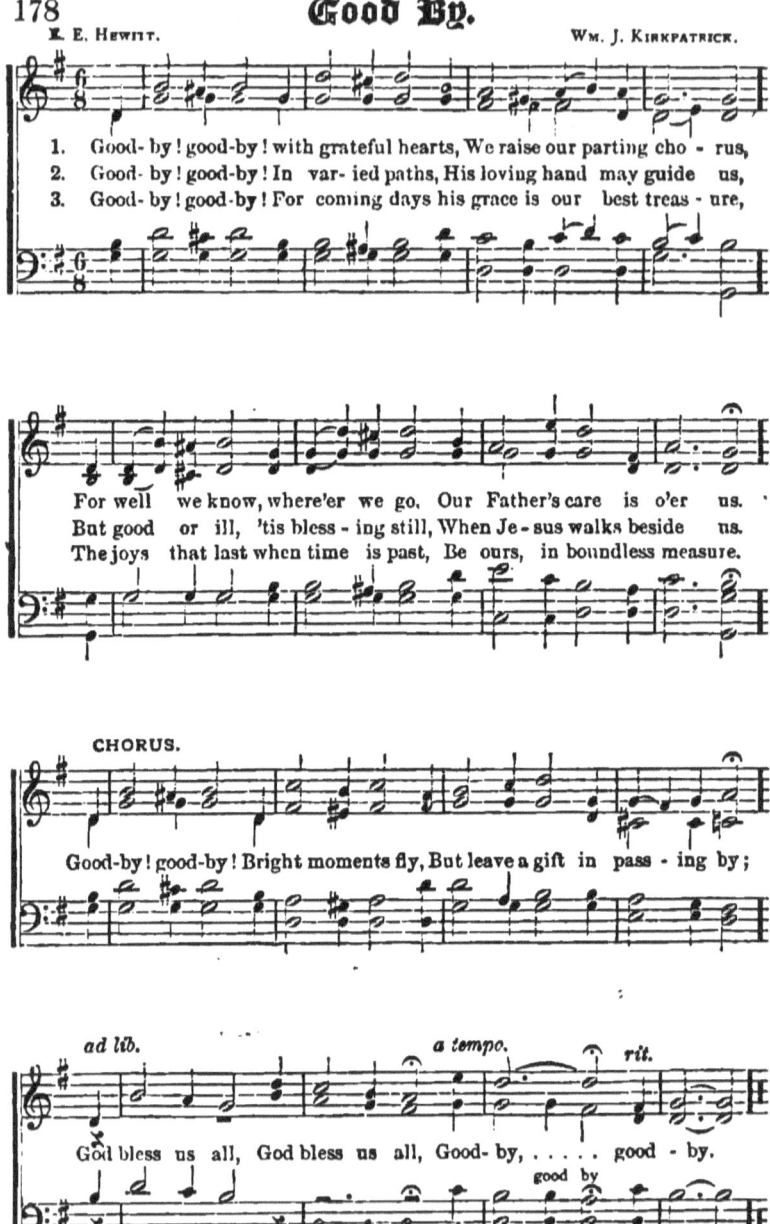

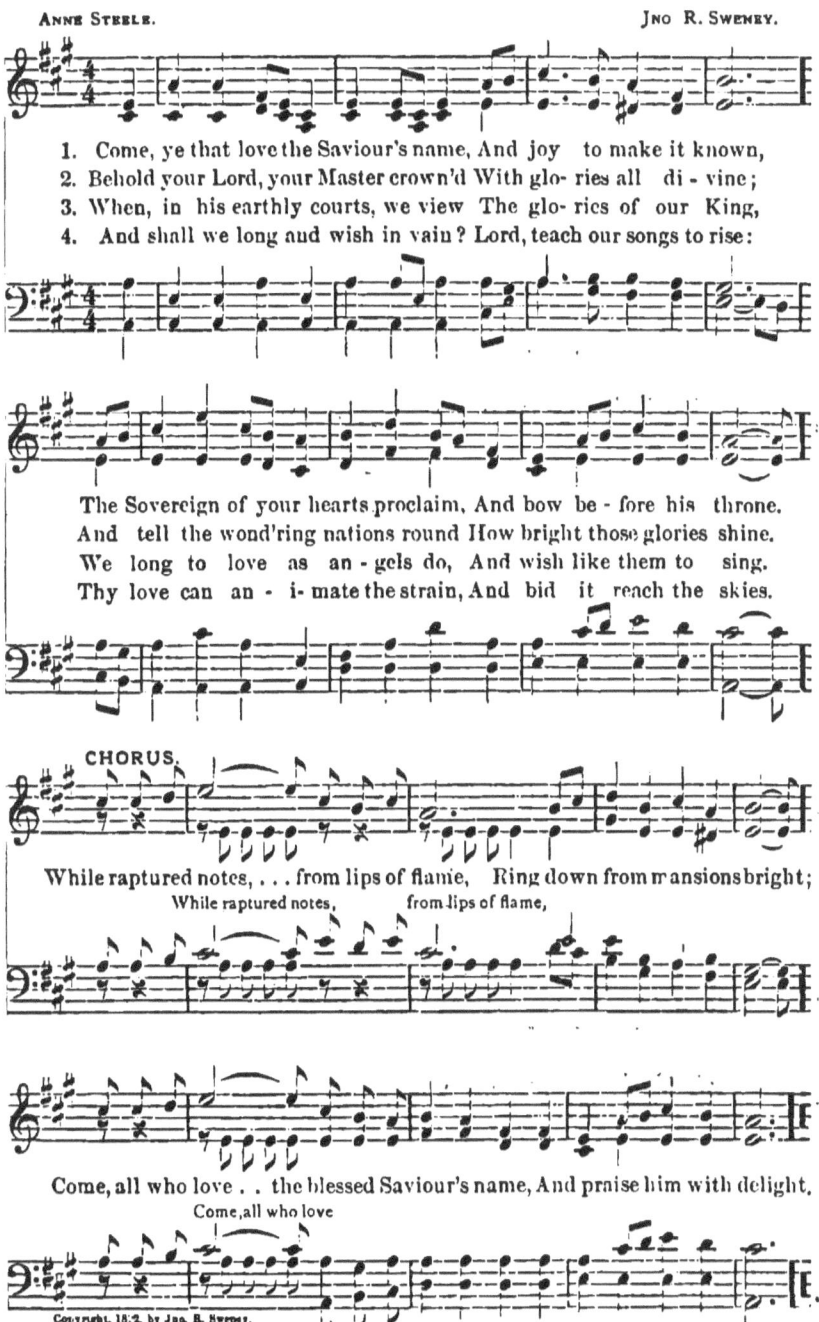

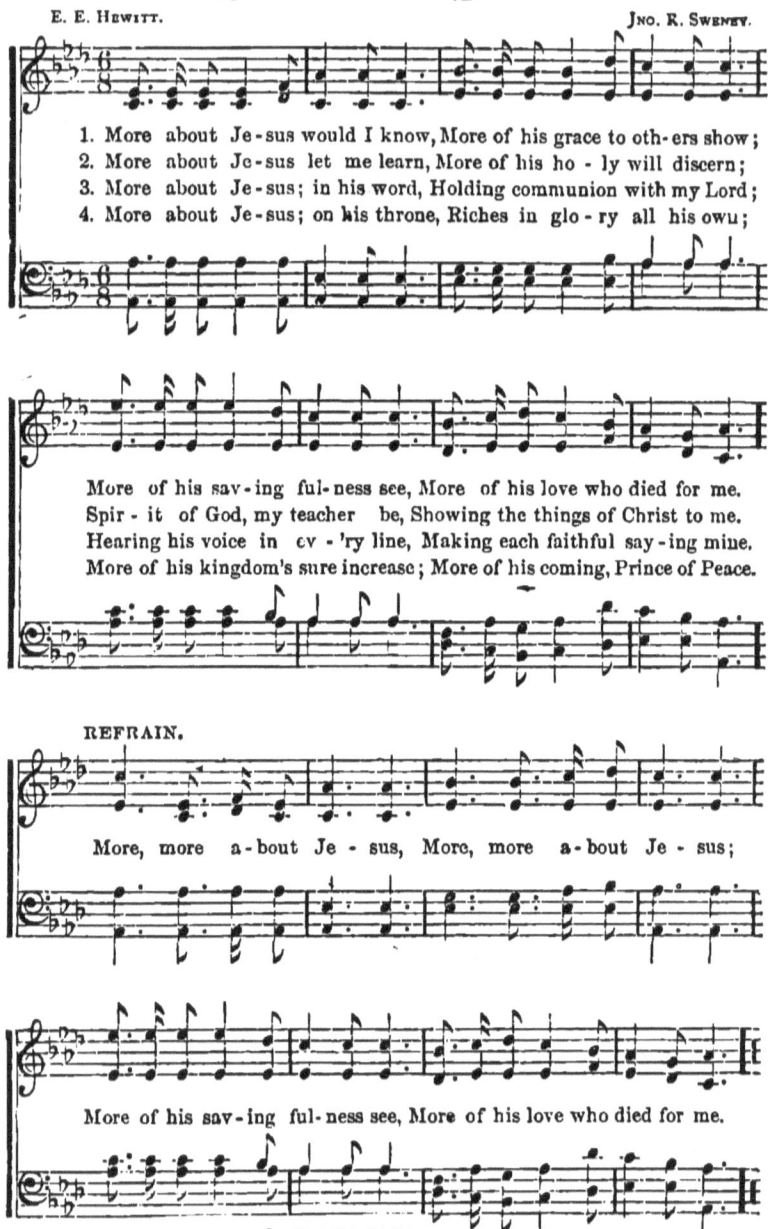

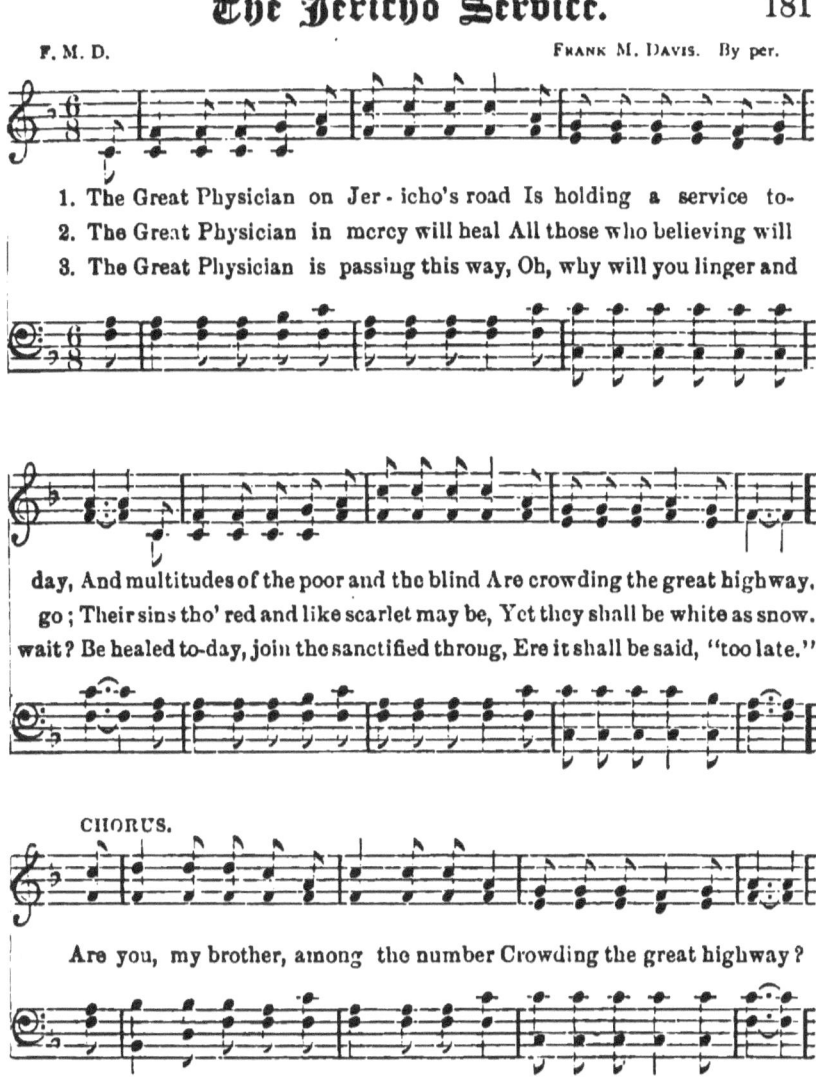

182. Jesus Saves Poor Sinners.

H. L. Gilmour. Matt. 1: 21. Plantation Melody. Arr. by H. L. G.

CHORUS.

Jesus saves, Jesus saves, Jesus saves poor sinners; Hear his call, "Come unto me,"
I'll give sweet rest from labor.
1. God lov'd poor sinners, And sent his Son to save them;
2. When tired and weary At Jacob's well he rested;
3. He touched a leper Who came to him beseeching,
4. Blind eyes were open'd, Deaf ears unstopp'd to hear him;
5. He saves believers When fully consecrat-ed,

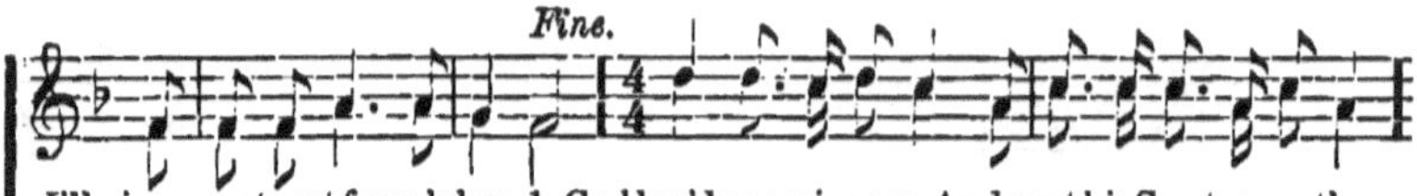

That who-so-ev-er trusts in him May now have life e-ter-nal.
A thirst-y women came to drink, He gave her liv-ing wa-ter.
"Lord if thou wilt, thou canst make clean," Immediate-ly he healed him.
The lame to walk and leap for joy, The dumb to shout his prais-es.
And faith makes good the promise true, The al-tar sanc-ti-fi-eth.

Copyright, 1892, by H. L. Gilmour.

183. Step Out on the Promise.

Maggie Potter. Arr. by E. F. M. E. F. Miller.

1. O mourner in Zi-on, how blessed art thou, For Je-sus is
2. O ye that are hun-gry and thirsty, re-joice! For ye shall be
3. Who sighs for a heart from in-i-qui-ty free? O poor, troubled
4. Step out on the promise, and Christ you shall win, "The blood of his

From "The Shout of Victory," by per.

Step Out on the Promise.—CONCLUDED.

wait- ing to com - fort thee now, Fear not to re - ly on the
filled; do you hear that sweet voice In - vit - ing you now to the
soul! there's a promise for thee, There's rest, weary one, in the
Son cleanseth us from all sin," It cleanseth me now, hal - le-

word of thy God; Step out on the promise,—get under the blood.
ban- quet of God? Step out on the promise,—get under the blood.
bos - om of God; Step out on the promise,—get under the blood.
lu - jah to God! I rest on his promise,— I'm under the blood.

184. The Excellent Way.

Rev. J. O. Foster.   Jno. R. Sweney.

1. { Which road are you going, my brother, What path are you treading to-day?
There's safety in one and no oth- er, And Christ is that excellent way.
2. { For wide is the gate to destruction, That opens for sinners to stray;
And many devoid of instruction Are going that dangerous way.

D.S.—safety in one and no oth- er, And Christ is that excellent way.

CHORUS.   D.S.

Which way,... which way,... Which way are you going to - day? There's
Which way,   which way,

Copyright, 1892, by Jno. R. Sweney.

3 The tones of the gospel are tender,
The love of the Master is strong;
Return to your God and surrender,
He's calling and waiting so long.

4 The promise is blessed and holy,
To all who will gladly obey;
And walk with the meek and the lowly
Along in the excellent way.

185 The Gospel Feast.

CHARLES WESLEY.
Cho. by H. L. G.
"Come, for all things are ready."
Luke xiv. 16.
H. L. GILMOUR.

1. Come, sinners, to the gos-pel feast; It is for you, it is for me;
2. Ye need not one be left behind, It is for you, it is for me;

Let ev'-ry soul be Je-sus' guest: It is for you, it is for me.
For God hath bid-den all mankind, It is for you, it is for me.

D.S.—O wea-ry wand'rer, come and see, It is for you, it is for me.

CHORUS.

Sal-va-tion full, sal-vation free, The price was paid on Calva-ry;

3 Sent by my Lord, on you I call;
  The invitation is to all:
4 Come, all the world! come, sinner, thou!
  All things in Christ are ready now.
5 Come, all ye souls by sin oppressed,
  Ye restless wanderers after rest;
6 Ye poor, and maimed, and halt, and blind
  In Christ a hearty welcome find.

7 My message as from God receive;
  Ye all may come to Christ and live:
8 O let this love your hearts constrain,
  Nor suffer him to die in vain.
9 See him set forth before your eyes,
  That precious, bleeding sacrifice:
10 His offered benefits embrace,
  And freely now be saved by grace.

Copyright, 1889, by H. L. Gilmour.

186 There is a fountain. Key A.

1 There is a fountain ||:fill'd with blood,:||
  Drawn from Immanuel's veins,
  And sinners, plunged ||:beneath that
    Lose all their guilty stains. [flood,:||
  CHO.—Oh, glorious fountain!
    Here will I stay,
    And in thee ever
    Wash my sins away.

2 The dying thief ||:rejoiced to see:||
  That fountain in his day,
  And there may I,||: though vile as he,:||
    Wash all my sins away.
3 Thou dying Lamb, ||: thy precious
    Shall never lose its power, [blood:||
  Till all the ransomed ||:Church of God:||
    Are saved to sin no more.
4 E'er since by faith ||: I saw the stream:||
    Thy flowing wounds supply,
  Redeeming love ||:has been my theme,:||
    And shall be till I die.

187. I'll Live for Him.

C. R. Dunbar.

1. My life, my love I give to thee, Thou Lamb of God, who died for me;
2. I now believe thou dost receive, For thou hast died that I might live;
3. Oh, thou who died on Cal-va-ry, To save my soul and make me free,

Cho.—I'll live for him who died for me, How happy then my life shall be!

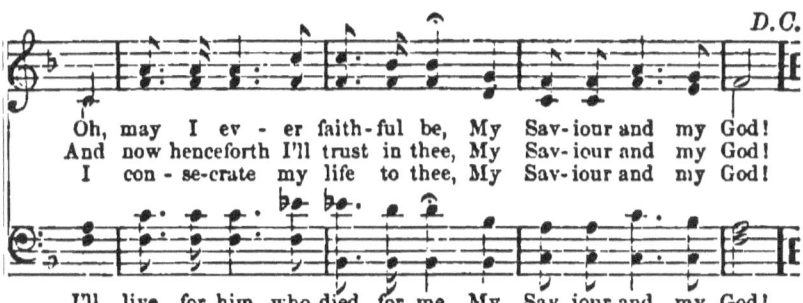

Oh, may I ev-er faith-ful be, My Sav-iour and my God!
And now henceforth I'll trust in thee, My Sav-iour and my God!
I con-se-crate my life to thee, My Sav-iour and my God!

I'll live for him who died for me, My Sav-iour and my God!

188. He is Calling.

Faber. Arr. by S. J. Vail.

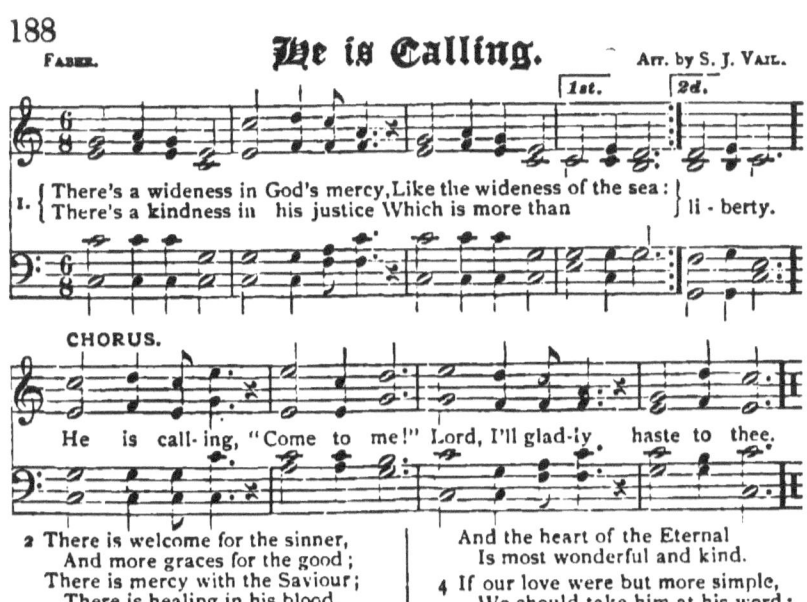

1. { There's a wideness in God's mercy, Like the wideness of the sea:
   There's a kindness in his justice Which is more than } li-ber-ty.

CHORUS.

He is call-ing, "Come to me!" Lord, I'll glad-ly haste to thee.

2 There is welcome for the sinner,
And more graces for the good;
There is mercy with the Saviour;
There is healing in his blood.

3 For the love of God is broader
Than the measure of man's mind:

And the heart of the Eternal
Is most wonderful and kind.

4 If our love were but more simple,
We should take him at his word;
And our lives would be all sunshine
In the sweetness of our Lord.

189. At the Cross.

R. Kelso Carter. From "Songs of Perfect Love," by per.

1. O Jesus, Lord, thy dying love Hath pierced my contrite heart;
2. Amid the night of sin and death Thy light hath filled my soul;
3. I kiss thy feet, I clasp thy hand, I touch thy bleeding side;
4. My Lord, my light, my strength, my all, I count my gain but loss;

Cho.—At the cross, at the cross, where I first saw the light,
And the burden of my heart rolled away,

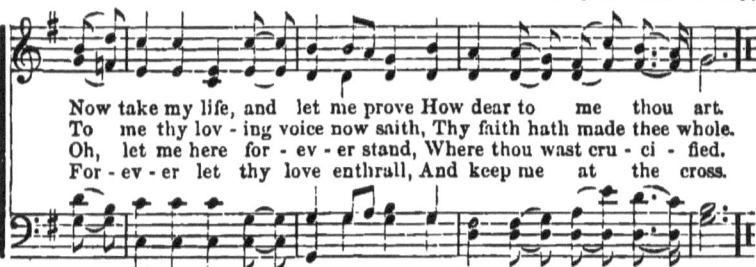

Now take my life, and let me prove How dear to me thou art.
To me thy loving voice now saith, Thy faith hath made thee whole.
Oh, let me here forever stand, Where thou wast crucified.
Forever let thy love enthrall, And keep me at the cross.

It was there by faith I received my sight, And now I am happy night and day!

190. Vain, Delusive World.

C. Wesley. Tune, PENITENCE.

1. Vain, delusive world, adieu, With all of creature good! Only Jesus I pursue,

D.S.—Only Jesus will I know,

Who bought me with his blood: All thy pleasures I forego;
And Jesus crucified.
I trample on thy wealth and pride;

2 Other knowledge I disdain;
'Tis all but vanity:
Christ, the Lamb of God, was slain,
He tasted death for me.
Me to save from endless woe
The sin-atoning Victim died:
Only Jesus will I know,
And Jesus crucified.

3 Here will I set up my rest;
My fluctuating heart
From the haven of his breast
Shall never more depart:
Whither should a sinner go?
His wounds for me stand open wide;
Only Jesus will I know,
And Jesus crucified.

4 Him to know is life and peace,
And pleasure without end;
This is all my happiness,
On Jesus to depend;
Daily in his grace to grow,
And ever in his faith abide;
Only Jesus will I know,
And Jesus crucified.

2 O that I could all invite,
This saving truth to prove;
Show the length, the breadth, the height,
And depth of Jesus' love!
Fain I would to sinners show
The blood by faith alone applied;
Only Jesus will I know,
And Jesus crucified.

91. Jesus, I Come to Thee.

Fanny J. Crosby. — Wm. J. Kirkpatrick.

1. Je-sus, I come to thee, Longing for rest; Fold thou thy wea-ry child Safe to thy breast. Rocked on storm-y sea,
2. Je-sus, I come to thee, Hear thou my cry; Save, or I per-ish, Lord, Save, or I die.
3. Now let the roll-ing waves Bend to thy will, Say to the troubled deep, Peace, peace, be still.
4. Swiftly the part-ing clouds Fade from my sight; Yon-der thy bow ap-pears, Love-ly and bright.

CHORUS.

Oh, be not far from me, Lord, let me cling to thee, On-ly to thee.

Copyright, 1894, by John J. Hood.

192. Nearer, My God! to Thee.

1 Nearer, my God! to thee,
Nearer to thee!
E'en though it be a cross
That raiseth me!
Still all my song shall be,
Nearer, my God! to thee,
Nearer to thee!

2 Though like the wanderer,
The sun gone down,
Darkness be over me,
My rest a stone,
Yet in my dreams I'd be
Nearer, my God! to thee,
Nearer to thee!

3 There let the way appear,
Steps unto heaven;
All that thou sendest me,
In mercy given;

Angels to beckon me
Nearer, my God! to thee,
Nearer to thee!

4 Then, with my waking thoughts
Bright with thy praise,
Out of my stony griefs
Bethel I'll raise;
So by my woes to be
Nearer, my God! to thee,
Nearer to thee!

5 Or if, on joyful wing
Cleaving the sky,
Sun, moon and stars forgot,
Upward I fly,
Still all my song shall be,
Nearer, my God! to thee,
Nearer to thee!

193. Use Me, Saviour.

Fred. Woodrow. / Chas. H. Gabriel.

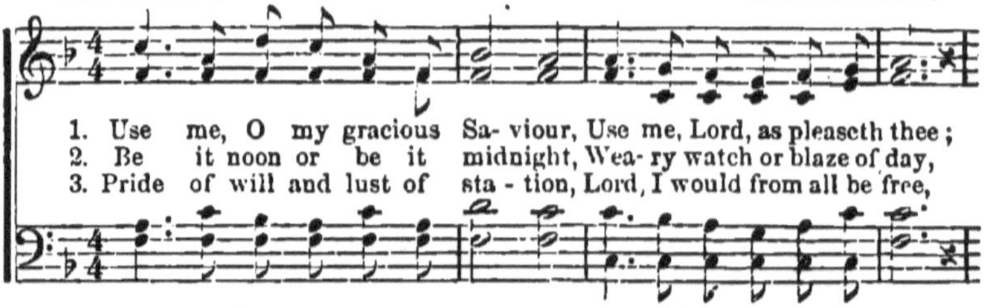

1. Use me, O my gracious Saviour, Use me, Lord, as pleaseth thee;
Nothing done for thee so lowly But is great enough for me.
2. Be it noon or be it midnight, Weary watch or blaze of day,
Shouting with the happy reapers, Toiling in the hidden way.
3. Pride of will and lust of station, Lord, I would from all be free,
And the only honor seeking, Lord, to be of use to thee.

CHORUS.

Use me, Use me, Use me as it pleaseth thee;
Use me, O my Saviour, Use me, O my Saviour,
Use me, Use me, Use me as it pleaseth thee.
Use me, O my Saviour, Use me, O my Saviour.

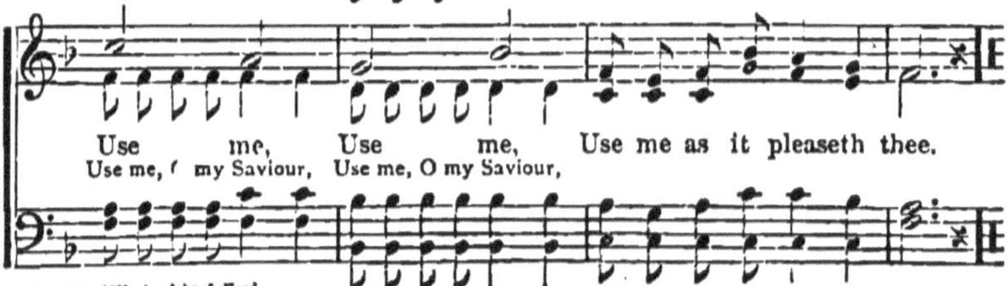

Copyright, 1891, by John J. Hood.

194. Happy On the Way.

John Cennick. / Arr. by W. J. K.

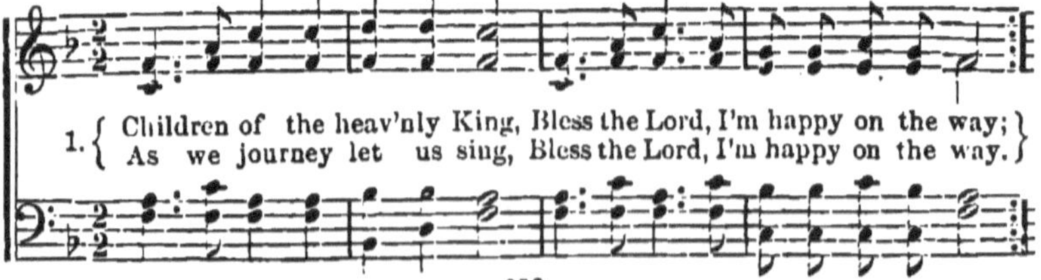

1. { Children of the heav'nly King, Bless the Lord, I'm happy on the way;
As we journey let us sing, Bless the Lord, I'm happy on the way. }

188

Happy On the Way.—CONCLUDED.

CHORUS.

Happy on the way, Happy on the way, Bless the Lord, I'm happy on the way.

1 Children of the heavenly King,
  As we journey let us sing.
2 Sing our Saviour's worthy praise,
  Glorious in his works and ways.
3 We are traveling home to God,
  In the way our father's trod;
4 They are happy now, and we
  Soon their happiness shall see.

5 Fear not, brethren, joyful stand
  On the borders of our land;
6 Jesus Christ, our Father's Son,
  Bids us undismayed go on.
7 Lord, obediently we'll go,
  Gladly leaving all below;
8 Only thou our leader be,
  And we still will follow thee.

195 O My Precious Saviour.

Mrs. C. N. Pickop.   Wm. J. Kirkpatrick.

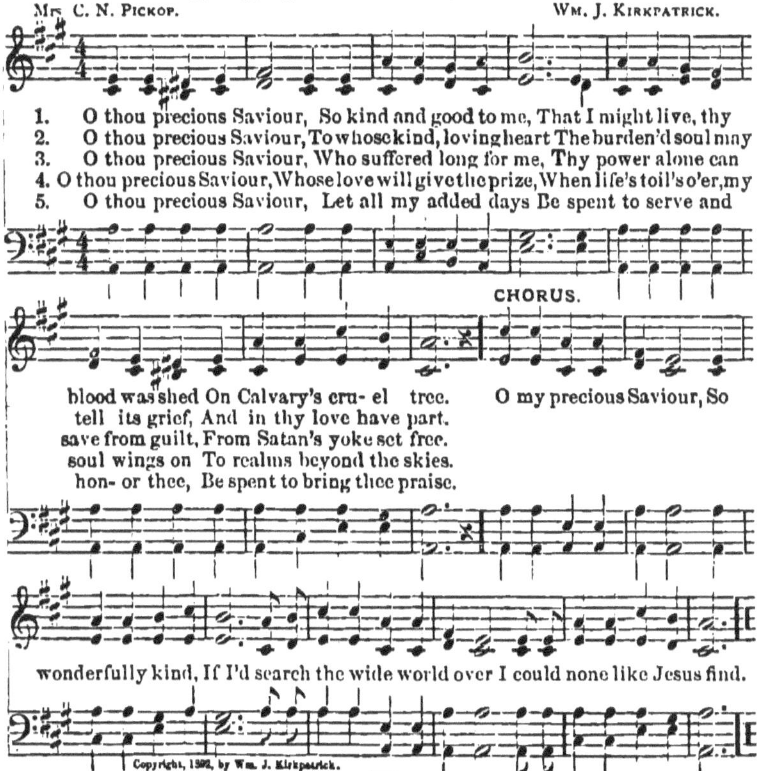

1. O thou precious Saviour, So kind and good to me, That I might live, thy
2. O thou precious Saviour, To whose kind, loving heart The burden'd soul may
3. O thou precious Saviour, Who suffered long for me, Thy power alone can
4. O thou precious Saviour, Whose love will give the prize, When life's toil's o'er, my
5. O thou precious Saviour, Let all my added days Be spent to serve and

CHORUS.

blood was shed On Calvary's cru- el tree.   O my precious Saviour, So
tell its grief, And in thy love have part.
save from guilt, From Satan's yoke set free.
soul wings on To realms beyond the skies.
hon- or thee, Be spent to bring thee praise.

wonderfully kind, If I'd search the wide world over I could none like Jesus find.

Copyright, 1892, by Wm. J. Kirkpatrick.

TOPICAL INDEX.

ASSURANCE, 102, 125, 165, 183.
AWAKENING, 162.
CHILDREN AND SUNDAY SCHOOL, 31, 78, 137.
CHRISTIAN ENDEAVOR, 144, 145, 164, 170, 193.
CONSECRATION, 99, 115, 187, 189, 190, 193.
COURAGE, 57, 103, 116, 172.
DEVOTION, 5, 35, 43, 46, 64, 73, 76, 139, 155, 191, 192.
EXHORTATION, 19, 44, 84, 107, 113, 160.
EXPERIENCE, 6, 16, 41, 69, 77, 79, 88, 99, 108.
FULL SALVATION, 1, 7, 9, 39, 80, 95, 100, 112, 114, 150, 169, 186, 190.
HEAVEN, 4, 13, 22, 30, 32, 38, 40, 49, 58, 81, 86, 92, 101, 142, 146, 148.
INVITATION, 12, 20, 63, 82, 96, 110, 119.
JESUS, 8, 14, 42, 51, 54, 65, 97, 99, 143, 153, 166, 167, 172, 175, 180, 184, 195.

JUDGEMENT, 134, 168.
MARCHING, 25, 26, 50, 105, 152.
MISCELLANEOUS, 127, 130, 151, 156.
MISSIONS, 158, 159.
PARDON, 28.
PENITENCE, 17, 18, 59, 71, 83, 91, 118, 141, 174.
PRAISE, 21, 23, 48, 53, 60, 66, 67, 72, 98, 128, 132, 149.
REJOICING, 29, 47, 70, 80, 94, 109, 121, 138, 194.
REST, 39, 51, 88, 120.
SECOND ADVENT, 10, 27, 87, 173.
TEMPERANCE, 147, 176, 177.
TESTIMONY, 45.
TRUST, 33, 34, 52, 55, 104, 106.
WORK AND PROMISE, 11, 15, 24, 36, 37, 56, 61, 68, 9), 111, 117, 122, 144.
WORSHIP, 136, 161.

INDEX.

Titles in CAPITALS; First lines in Roman.

	HYMN.		HYMN.		HYMN.
Abiding in the shadow	69	Good-by! good-by!	178	I WILL TRUST IN MY	55
ALL BRIGHT ABOVE,	16	GO YE INTO ALL THE	159	I wonder who is the	78
ANCHOR ME HOME,	130	Graciously, tenderly,	130		
A PERFECT REST. .	39	Great is Jehovah,	161	Jesus, and shall ever be,.	172
A PERFECT SALVATION,	114			JESUS COMES,.	173
A pierced hand is knock-	107	HAND IN HAND WITH	79	JESUS FOR ME,	99
A PLACE FOR THEE,	124	HAPPY IN A SAVIOUR'S.	94	Jesus, I come to thee,	191
Are we doing for the Mas-	37	Happy in the Lord my	29	Jesus is keeping my soul	112
Are we sowing, with a	117	HAPPY ON THE WAY,	194	JESUS IS PASSING BY,	82
Are you getting ready,	134	HASTEN TO THE FOUN-.	119	JESUS, MY SAVIOUR,	153
Are you sitting idle?	164	HASTE WITH THE LIFE-	36	Jesus, my Saviour, is all.	99
ASHAMED OF JESUS,	172	Hast thou a treasure in	104	Jesus my Saviour to	175
A SHELTER IN THE	65	HAVE COURAGE TO SAY	44	Jesus, O thou loving	97
As here we come to	48	Have you ever heard the	166	JESUS RECEIVETH SIN-.	18
A sinner was wandering.	162	Heartily, heartily, ,	122	JESUS SAVES POOR SIN-.	182
A TALK ABOUT JESUS,	42	Hear ye not the Saviour.	140	Jesus, Saviour, oh, how	106
AT THE CROSS,	189	HE IS CALLING,	188	JESUS, SHEPHERD,	97
Away beyond the stars	12	HE IS JUST THE SAME	166	JESUS THE CHILDREN'S.	78
		HE'LL MENTION THEM,	28	Jesus the loving Shep-	20
BEHOLD I STAND AND	107	HE OPENED MY EYES,	108	JESUS WILL WELCOME.	58
BE NOT AFRAID; 'TIS I,	103	Here a little, and there a	56		
Be strong, O ye faithful,.	24	HE'S WITH ME ALL THE	77	KEPT IN PERF. PEACE,.	69
Blessed joys of God be-.	138	How oft have we heard	110	KEEP THE FAITH,.	156
Blessed life in Jesus,	121	HOW OFT WE ARE.	30	KEEP THOU ME,	106
Bless the Lord! praise	98	How oft would I have	63	KIND WORDS ARE AL-.	145
BLEST, BLEST FOREVER	13	How precious the thought	40		
Bravely launch the tem-.	177	How sweet 'twould be	103	Lead me, my Saviour; .	64
BREATHE UPON US,	155	Hungry, Lord, for thy	1	LEND A HAND,	164
BROTHER, WILL YOU GO	12			Let children hear the	31
		I am bowed at the cross.	80	Let us counsel,	42
Children of the heavenly	194	I am feeding on the	75	LET US EXALT THE	48
CLOSE THY HEART NO.	84	I am learning a song that	128	Life wears a different	41
Come, contrite one, and.	82	I am not skilled to un-	167	Like a bird on the deep,.	174
Come in, come into the .	131	I am walking to-day in	150	Look up to Jesus, lift up	144
Come, O come with an-.	53	I came to the Master in,	6	Lord, have mercy, oh,	71
Come, sinners, to the	185	I gave my life for thee,	160	LORD, I'M COMING	141
COME TO THE FEAST,	135	I HAVE COME TO THE	169	LOVINGLY, TENDERLY.	20
Come ye that love the	179	I have heard my Saviour	91		
Crowned with glory, and	154	I have precious news to.	47	MARCHING ON TO CAN-	152
		I have surrendered to	115	MARCHING TO JERUSA-	25
Dear Saviour, take this	35	I hear of a city that's	108	MARCHING TO VICTORY	105
		I'LL EVER HOLD ON TO.	62	Marching with gladness.	50
ENOUGH AND TO SPARE	96	I'LL LIVE FOR HIM,	187	March, march away to	26
		I long to be perfect, my .	139	MERCY IS BOUNDLESS	157
FAIR PORTALS,	86	In dreams I hear a song.	32	More about Jesus would	180
Fearless and faithful,	66	In realms of bliss, where	124	MORE AND MORE,.	73
Fear not the foes advance	57	IN THE MASTER'S NAME	117	MOUNTAINS OF BEU-	100
FEAR THOU NOT, .	116	IN THE SERVICE OF	90	My soul is full of glad-.	77
FED UPON THE FINEST.	1	In the twilight of the	76	My soul sings glory all	28
FOLLOW ALL THE WAY	91	I see the bright, effulgent	16	My life, my love, I give.	187
For thy goodness, O my.	73	I SHALL BE SATISFIED,.	101	MY SAVIOUR,	167
		It is not time that flies,	127	MY SONG OF JOY, .	128
Give glory to Jesus, who	149	IT WILL NEVER GROW	146		
GLORY, HE SAVES!	9	I've clasped the powerful	79	Nearer, my God, to thee,	192
Glory to Jesus, he saves.	9	I've heard of streets of	4	Nearer to thy side, dear.	43
Go forth, go forth, tho'	11	I've wandered far away .	141	Never will the Lord for-.	52
Going home to be with	148	I was once far away	169	NONE LIKE HIM, .	8
GO IN PEACE,.	6	I will sing of him who	67	Now I have found at Je-	39

191

WINNING SONGS.

Title	#	Title	#	Title	#
O for a heart that is	5	SWEET REST THERE,	40	'TWILL ALL BE RIGHT	46
O have you not heard of	146	Swing back for one mo-	86		
Oh, blessed cross of Je-	101			Under thy shadow abid-	125
Oh, come to feast on the	135	Take courage, temper-	176	UNSEARCHABLE RICH-	143
Oh, how can we sail over	36	TAKE THIS HEART OF	35	Use me, O my gracious	193
Oh, praise the dear Sav-	100	TELL HIS GOODNESS	53		
Oh, speak kind words	145	TELL THEM NOW,	37	Vain, delusive world, a-	190
Oh, tell the world that	23	Tell the world of Jesus,	158		
Oh, the tender love of	54	Thank God for the foun-	72	WAITING FOR PARDON,	59
O Jesus, Lord, thy dying	189	Thanks be to Jesus, his	157	WAITING TO FORGIVE,	140
O mourner in Zion,	183	THAT MEETING TO	134	WASHED IN THE BLOOD	80
O MY PRECIOUS SAV-	195	The banquet hall is rich-	18	Watch and pray that	87
O my Saviour and Re-	85	The blood of the Saviour	95	Watch, ye saints, with	173
On a travel-worn road,	74	THE CHILDREN'S SAV-	31	We are drifting towards	81
Only a little while sowing	13	THE EXCELLENT WAY,	184	We are marching along,	105
ONLY DO RIGHT,	147	THE FOLD OF LOVE,	75	We are marching on to	152
ON THE JERICHO ROAD	74	THE GOSPEL FEAST,	185	We are marching to Jeru-	25
O the unsearchable rich-	143	The great Physician on	181	Weary child thy sin for-	84
O they tell me of a home	142	THE HOME LAND OF	49	WE ARE NEARING,	81
O thou precious Saviour	195	THE JERICHO SERVICE,	181	We come, we come,	137
Our friends on earth we	171	The joy of his salvation,	109	WE HAVE AN ANCHOR,	165
Out in the breakers are	15	THE LORD IS KING,	23	WELCOME FOR ME,	174
Over the river they call	58	THE LORD REIGNETH,	21	WE'LL BE THERE SOME	4
O what must I do to be	17	The Lord's our rock, in	65	WE'LL BUILD ON THE	14
		THE MUSIC OF THE H.	89	WE'LL NEVER BE A-	57
PERFECT IN THEE,	139	The music springs within	89	WE'LL NEVER SAY G.	171
Plant roses, sweet roses,	68	There is a fountain filled	186	We sing of a land where	30
PRAISE HIM WITH DE-	179	There is plenty in Jesus,	96	WE WILL FOLLOW ON,	61
Pray on, pray on,	46	There rolled thro' time	21	What a shout the ran-	38
PUT YOUR TRUST IN	33	THE ROSE OF SHARON,	154	WHAT MUST I DO TO BE	17
		There's a great day com-	168	What sayest thou of Je-	19
Rejoicing evermore in	70	There's a rose that is	154	What shall I do with Je-	83
Resting, sweetly resting	88	There's a song in my	132	When I shall wake in	101
Rest, weary heart,	51	There's a spring of joy	90	When looking o'er life's	8
Revive, O Lord, our	155	There's a wideness in	188	When my spirit droops	116
		There's a word for me in	126	When on clouds of glory	27
SAFE AT HOME,	38	THE SCARLET LINE,	95	When the hosts redeemed	92
SAVE ONE,	15	The sea may be rough	62	When the sheep have all	22
Saviour, dear, I have	59	THE SHEPHERD'S FOLD	22	Where the Saviour's	61
SAVIOUR, I'M TRUSTING	34	THE SIMPLE, EARNEST	76	Which road are you go-	184
Saviour, we come to thee	120	THE SINNER AND THE	162	While Jesus is calling,	44
SEARCHING FOR ME,	175	THE SWEET BEULAH	150	While we walk by faith	94
Send out the sunlight,	111	THE TEMP. LIFE-BOAT,	177	Who laid his native glory	153
SHOUTING HIS PRAISE,	66	THE UNCLOUDED DAY,	142	Will your anchor hold in	165
SINCE I FOUND MY SAV-	41	THEY THAT SOW IN	11	With a perfect salvation,	114
Sing and rejoice in re-	60	THIS I DID FOR THEE,	160	With tearful eyes I look,	129
Sinner, fear not, Jesus	119	Tho' the shadows gather	55	Witnesses for Jesus, tell,	45
SOME HAPPY DAY,	32	Thou, whose all-prevad-	136	Wonderful songs of sal-	151
SOUL REST,	120	Thro' the world, with	156	Wonderful words of sal-	34
Speak a good word for	113	TIME AND ETERNITY,	127	WONDROUS LOVE,	85
SPEAK FOR THE MAS-	113	'Tis a faithful saying,	7	WONDROUSLY RED'MED	47
SPEED ON,	176	'TIS MURMURING LOW,	110	WRECK AND RESCUE,	118
Spread the light of joy a-	123	'Tis not a land unknown,	49	Wrecked and struggling.	118
STEP OUT ON THE PR.	189	'Tis the purpose of love,	14		
STEPPING IN THE LIGHT	170	'TIS WELL, 'TIS WELL,	104	Ye messengers of grace,	159
SURRENDERED,	115	Trust God as a child of	33	Yes, for me, for me he	10
Sweet assurance, thou	102	Trying to walk in the	170	YE WOULD NOT,	63

www.ingramcontent.com/pod-product-compliance
Lightning Source LLC
Chambersburg PA
CBHW032138160426
43197CB00008B/700